MW00803610

Fossils

William Arthur Hammer (posthumously)

and

Jennifer Ann Cataline

For Fuji

*Some names have been changed for privacy

Table of Contents

PREFACE

Listen. . . I have something to tell you. This is the story of my husband. His life, our marriage, his death, my grief, and my rebirth. I still don't know what it all means. But I know it matters.

Bill and I started writing this book together in 2000. Eventually we fell in love and like other things, it was put in a drawer and forgotten. When he was diagnosed with Lung Cancer in 2009 he pulled it back out and worked on it for as long as he could. Inevitably he became too weak to write, type, and then dictate. I promised I would finish it; I keep my promises.

Though an amazing story teller, my husband was not much of a writer. His hopes for this book were that some addict somewhere would be spared the pain his alcoholism and addiction cost him and his family. Bill spent the last twenty years of his life clean and sober. He dedicated himself entirely to helping others achieve similar goals.

For me, his story--our story--is about much more. It's one of forgiveness, acceptance, discovery, unconditional love--letting go. And other things too immense and impalpable to even try to classify.

One year has passed since Bill died and I resumed writing the book. Today I will finish it. I would not even know where to start in thanking the many people who helped us when he was sick and those who have been here for me in the last year as I struggled to rebuild a life without him. Medical professionals, friends, family, neighbors, long-lost class mates, college professors, and strangers: I had forgotten how many good people were out there until Bill got sick. They helped me remember. And I really needed that.

I can spend the rest of my life mourning Bill's death. But it would serve no purpose. So instead, I have decided to spend it celebrating his life. His gifts. His lessons. There were so many. Bill taught me things I had no idea I needed to learn. It is because of him that I now know if I am never loved again it will not matter, because I was not put here to be loved. I was put here to love.

I was put here *to* love. What a blessing.

I hope you let yourself come to love Bill. God knows I did.

LETTER

Dear Bill,

Yesterday I ate four pieces of pumpkin pie. It rained. Thanksgiving exploded and fizzled like a firework and the turkey you didn't carve is digesting in my stomach.

I expected to wake up hateful this morning, unable to expose even a limb to the chilly November air. Thinking perhaps breathing alone would require all my energy and my comforter could wrap me up like a burrito, making getting out of bed an impossible and unnecessary task. I was wrong. The best kind of wrong you can be.

Miraculously, Bill, I am surviving. Another holiday has come and gone, and I am still here. I don't know what I thought would happen, but it hasn't. I've survived our anniversary, a change of season, a relapse earlier in the month . . . and I'm making it. Sometimes the sun still shines and coffee still tastes good.

I know you help me. I knew last Sunday when I awoke around 2:00 a.m. to the sound of your music box playing mysteriously from the other room that you were helping me.

You died three months ago. I am a small pink and blond girl preparing to lose my teeth one at a time. I can taste the blood on my tongue as I probe around in my mouth. My school pictures will reveal a sad smile with gaps where teeth had been. But this time I know new ones will grow in.

It's time to start letting you go, dear husband. A bit at a time . . . like sipping hot cocoa. No gulping.

I miss you Bill. And I love you.

Love, your adoring wife--Jenn

INTRODUCTION

My husband was a complicated man. Not better or worse than any other man, just complicated.

An endless pool of compassion, he extended an ocean of courtesy, a limitless fountain of kindness to others that he was frequently unable to give himself. He never quite believed he had earned his space on our planet. Bill derived his self worth primarily from his occupations. He once said "Being a cop made my self-esteem tolerable."

He was never good enough for himself. Bill was 19 years, four months, and two weeks clean and sober when he was diagnosed with small cell Lung cancer. It was terminal. Deep down, Bill believed the punishment for his sins had finally found him, invaded his body, grabbed hold with an angry fervor and determined itself to make him pay.

In the months following his diagnosis he wrote "My greatest sin has always been not being there for my children. I missed out on a lot of wonderful times when they were growing up. My family suffered greatly from my ill-fated choices. My absence both from them and society was disgraceful."

The nine months and one week he lived following that fateful day was a journey he embarked upon with great moderation and balance--sometimes fighting for his life, sometimes struggling to make sense of it, and sometimes setting himself to the task of leaving a legacy that would make our lives easier. God how I loved him for it. "I need to clear my mind now" he would say before getting lost in his writing. "Otherwise I miss out on the opportunity to do something right for someone else."

A natural introvert and intensely private man, my husband did not require apologies and rarely gave them himself. Quick to forgive and harboring few grudges, Bill said simply, "How can we make this better?" when he had caused harm. Only since his death have I been able to appreciate the beauty and health in his strategy. Bill despised being punished and refused to punish those who had damaged their relationship with him. "If I know the truth, what does it matter?" He was right about so many things.

I met Bill on the eighteenth anniversary of the death of John Lennon. Having just graduated with my Master of Arts degree in Counseling, I accepted my first position as a Chemical Dependency Counselor in Tiffin, a neighbor to my hometown of Findlay, Ohio. It was a cold December 8, 1998 and already dark when my new supervisor, during a tour of the building, led me into the dimly lit staff break room. Almost 6:00 p.m., most employees had gone for the night and Bill, in his beige coat and glasses, was himself heading toward the back door.

"Bill, this is our new CD therapist, Jennifer Cataline" announced my supervisor as Bill and I shook hands.

"Nice to meet you" he said. My hand felt such relief in his. Like it had lain down in his palm for a much-needed nap. I liked him immediately.

A soft-spoken and gentle man, Bill had a calm, quiet way about him. Two office doors down from mine, he was a constant anchor in a frequently stormy sea of angry clients and burned-out colleagues.

His smile shy and secretive, his walk more of a stride than individual steps, his body a perfectly unassuming but well maintained frame for housing his conflicted self, I eventually fell in love with him.

Bill was equal parts cocky, confident, arrogant, evolved, insecure, humble, scared, ashamed, needy, vulnerable, self-contained, lonely, and dignified; damn he was one fine-looking man. His hugs warm and sincere, his kisses owning and desperate, he was the sexiest man I've ever known.

In August 2003 we bought our first and only home together. We exchanged our vows there on the patio beside the pool on the thirtieth of that month while Etta James crooned "At Last." Bill must have said "that was the happiest day of my life" one hundred times during our marriage. Those words wrap a soft comforter around my heart on damp, windy, autumn days like today. Days when I would give up everything to hold his hand one more time.

VERA

Vera came to us in late September, 2009. A full bred Blue Great Dane, she had been abandoned by her original owner. Left chained in his back yard when he moved, underweight, rampant with infections, and inadequately socialized, Vera was a truly docile and gentle soul. I loved her.

After weeks of vet trips, antibiotics, ear drops, flea baths, and adequate nutrition, Vera started coming to life. "I'm gonna get your ball, Vera! I'm gonna get it!" I played with her in our spacious back yard. Vera could fit her entire orange rubber ball, similar in size to a volleyball, in her mouth. Nothing pleased her more than a good game of Keep-Away.

It was while playing her favorite game that Vera, in her exuberance, leapt up to retrieve her ball, which Bill held just above his head. "I wouldn't do that if I were..." I didn't have time to finish my sentence. She landed squarely on Bill's sternum, firmly planting her massive right paw on him and, with it, the bulk of her weight. She took all his air.

Nothing was ever the same again.

Assuming his subsequent symptoms were all related to that injury, my husband suffered constant nausea, weight loss, breathing difficulty, coughing up blood, insomnia, and what I can only imagine was unbearable pain while he was "doctored" himself using only Ibuprofen and Alka Seltzer to treat a diagnosis of Xyphoiditis.

On the first Wednesday in November, I'd had enough and began making phone calls. My husband was deteriorating and his abdomen swollen like a pregnant woman in her second trimester. He was scheduled to see a colleague that Friday morning for a second opinion.

When my husband left his office on Thursday November 5, 2009, we did not know it would be his last day of work. We did not know it would be the last day of life as we knew it.

BLACKIE

The details of my father's absence in my life the summer I was four are sketchy. Originally, my mother said he returned to Fostoria, Ohio to find work. I have heard many stories. He quit his job as a manager of a grocery store after a "disagreement" with my mother. A Dr. Bernard told him he had developed a bleeding ulcer and prescribed some "nerve pills." Blah, blah, blah and who really knows. In any event, his leave taking in my life was marked by the presence of a puppy he gave me as a gift. Blackie was a black and white terrier mix named after a TV suspense show called "Boston Blackie."

We lived in a suburb outside of Detroit with my maternal grandmother, Nana. I loved Nana. The first grandchild, she and my aunts set out to spoil me in ways my own mother never would. My aunt loves to tell the story of the time she called our house that summer and I answered the phone. "What are you doing today?" she asked me. "Oh," I said, real casual like, "just rewaxing and watching uncow Miwty." In contrast, my mother enjoyed waiting for an audience in which to embarrass me. She winded and looked around at everyone, "Now Billy, say banana," knowing damn well I could not say banana.

Standing about five feet five inches tall Nana was a gentle, yet hardworking woman with a big gray bun and lovely wrinkle-free face. She managed a laundromat and collected social security from the death of my grandfather, to diverticulitis, about ten years before. As the oldest, this left my mother to take over many responsibilities of the house. She described this year of her life, at the age of 12, as "the end of any fun." I recall feeling ashamed of my mother while I was still quite young. She did not give pillowy hugs like Nana and rarely smiled. Though not unattractive, my mother was not a beautiful woman. In my childhood naiveté I often thought if my mother had been beautiful she would love me better. Later I realized it was the beauty

missing from her own life which prevented her from being a better mother to me.

The home Nana rented in the suburbs was not one she could have afforded alone. Nana's

boyfriend financed the rest. Uncle Sid was a big man with wavy auburn hair who wore pin

striped bib overalls and an engineer hat. He worked for the railroad. Although he never

misbehaved in my presence, he was rarely seen without a Stroh's gripped firmly in his hand. He

fascinated me with the chug-chug-chug-chug-choo-choo sound he made on his harmonica.

While Uncle Sid spent a lot of time with us, he did not live at Nana's house. As evening settled

in, the man always appeared to have someplace else he was supposed to be. My two year old

sister was the other inhabitant of Nana's that summer. Consequently, I dreaded the departure of

the only other man in the house.

"Uncow Sid" I'd say in my little kid way, "Do you really have to go now?"

My mother usually hissed from somewhere behind me "He's not your uncle."

Then off he went into the sunset.

Few trees dotted the landscape of the neighborhood in which we lived. There were no

bushes in the yards and grass almost as sparse since the construction of this subdivision had only

been completed several months prior. The greatest joy in my life was Blackie. He was my best

friend and constant companion. Blackie was my only link to my father.

I spent many hot afternoons in Detroit that summer teaching Blackie how to play fetch.

He clenched the stick in his jaws and came galloping back all proud and panting to have pleased

me. We rolled on the ground and he kissed my flushed face with his pink tongue. After he was

finally potty trained, Nana gave the okay that he could sleep with me.

In the mornings we crawled out of bed together and pitter pattered our way across the linoleum kitchen floor to the side door. My mother yelled "keep him on that leash" before the screen door slammed behind me. As soon as we rounded the corner of the red brick house I took the leash off and he went to the bathroom wherever he wanted to in that yard. That made the landlord, who lived next door, squeeze his beady eyes tight before shaking his head side to side and storming back into his house. Blackie didn't pay him any mind.

We passed the summer away together like that. It was the summer before I was to start kindergarten. What would Blackie do without me in the mornings while I went to school?

One late autumn Sunday afternoon we returned home after visiting several members of my mother's immediate family who lived in the Detroit area. As always, I was the first to hop eagerly out of the car and run joyfully into the side door to greet Blackie. Although he was allowed to sleep in my room at night, he had to stay in the basement when we were gone. On that occasion, I got to the basement door and nudged with the typical force. But the door did not open. I pushed it again and nothing happened. I tried and tried and pushed harder and harder and finally opened the door just enough to squeeze the top of half of my body through the crack to look behind.

Lying motionless on the landing behind the door was my best friend, Blackie. At that moment a larger and stronger body than mine pushed the door open further, grabbed my tiny body, and pulled me away. A voice sounding distant and hollow, though recognizable as Uncle Sid's, told me to "go in the other room son."

I felt lost in the big beige couch of the usually comfortable living room.

Muffled voices traveled the hallways and bounced off the painted sandy woodwork.

"That Goddamned son of a bitch . . . he must have poisoned him . . . ", "It's not like we weren't allowed to have a dog . . ." That went on for some bit of time. I don't really remember. I remember only that I was scared and confused. I wanted Blackie to wake up and lick my face. I wanted him to hop into my bed and curl into my tummy.

That night I cried myself to sleep. No one told me it was okay to feel sad. No one told me it was okay to feel anything.

No one told me it was okay to miss those we love who go away and don't tell us where they're going or when they're coming home.

LETTER

Dear Bill,

Just out of my reach are the words to tell you how desperately I don't want this to be happening. Like watching something awful on TV but the remote is lost. The channel of my life cannot be changed. My anger has grown so big, so disproportionate to my capacity to contain it, it has burst me open at my seams. The pain oozes. It seeps into everything. My dreams when I sleep. My steps when I walk. My hands when I hold. My eyes when I see.

An avalanche has stolen the ground from under me, Bill. I have not stopped tumbling. I am wholly and utterly lost without you.

I want to feel you behind me in the spring at the rushing river, your hands around my waist.

I want to bury my nose in your neck, wrap myself around your warm body on Christmas Eve while you watch Mass on the Toledo station and the tree lights blink new chances.

I want to feed you sweet bites of sticky elephant ear at the Hancock County fair while we swat at fearless bees.

I want to dive into the cool, clean water of our pool, swim to you and cling forever to your sturdy arms.

One year ago today you were diagnosed with small cell carcinoma and started chemo. I am sorry I didn't tell you more often how brave I thought you were.

I miss you.

Love, your adoring wife- Jenn

HOSTAGES

The first time Bill told me how afraid he had been most of his life we were naked at the Super 8 Motel. Resting comfortably on my left side, I watched the smoke from my cigarette dance between my long red nails, and listened intently to the conviction in his steady voice. "I earned you, Jennifer," he asserted. "I survived a lot, waded through a lot to get to you." It reminded me of how Newton may have sounded had the Catholic Church apologized in a more timely manner.

From the chair beside the bed, he leaned over me. He kissed my forehead, my cheek, my lips, my chin, my neck. My skin tingled. It was the most alive I had ever felt. At times his words landed on me like a soft breeze and at others like a deep tissue massage on aching muscles. It felt good no matter how much some of it hurt.

I had no idea then how heavy those words weighed on his heart, that they were tattooed on him like an anchor on the arm of a sailor. I had no clue this fine man, so seemingly confidant, had spent most of his waking moments afraid, and would one day be my husband.

I knew only that I had fallen in love with this wounded man, and he with me. Bill was 54 years old that Sunday Afternoon in May. I was 30.

We chiseled away at each other like sculptors until all we needed of each other was left. Two beautiful, flawed, porcelain-skinned people . . . half clothed, frozen in that moment, adored with our missing limbs.

I can still see the way a shaft of light crept in at the edge of the thick, heavy curtains and bounced off the mirror in that motel room . . . the way the brown polyester blanket crumpled at my ankles on the bed like small hills . . . the way his face transformed from my colleague to my lover.

It is harder now to imagine him any other way. The year before Bill got clean and sober I had just graduated from high school. Bill was already older then than I am now, his widow.

Running out of money, being late, not paying a bill on time, being grabbed by the arm or leg, being confined or cornered, small spaces, looking incompetent in front of others, heavy traffic, God, Hell, getting angry, intimacy, being revealed, being alone, missing a deadline, hospitals, doctors, germs, looking like a fool, being perceived as unclean, the list of things my husband feared revealed themselves starting that day and continued coming throughout the duration of our marriage. They tethered him to a pole like a ball.

As a result, Bill described his antics during his earlier marriages including infidelity, abuse, staying out for days on end, wrecking cars, breaking promises, sucking up all the family resources . . . the list went on. He referred to all three of his prior wives as "hostages" and once said "the smartest thing any of them ever did was to get the hell away from me." He did not know how to liberate himself. Bill thought by enslaving others, he could avoid feeling trapped himself. He didn't realize how wrong he was until much later.

This is not the uncle my niece Raye ever saw. Raye knew an uncle who came to her dance recitals with flowers. This is not the papa his granddaughters Susan and Samantha ever saw. Susan and Samantha knew a papa who cooked them hot dogs on the grill at pool parties. This is not the father figure my best friend Fuji ever saw. Fuji knew a father figure who worked side by side with her on home repair projects and called her his "little helper." This is not the brother-in-law my sister Jodi or her husband Tim ever saw. They knew a brother-in-law who could always be counted on for a good game of Texas Hold 'Em. I never met that man myself . . . the one who had hostages instead of wives. Bill gave me the freedom I spent my lifetime seeking. He loved me until I knew how to love myself.

No, we never met that other man. But we knew Bill. And we all loved him.

MY FIRST VACATION

My first marriage was a shotgun wedding as I had impregnated my high school sweetheart, Julie, our senior year. Our Catholic administration, which loved us both so dearly, responded kindly by expelling us from school.

I thought I was deeply in love with my first wife. Now I realize I didn't know the meaning of love and still struggle, though I have a much firmer grasp on it. I just wanted someone to touch me and teach me I was worth something.

After we were married for about ten years it became evident things weren't going well. With that in mind, we decided to take our first vacation to a dude ranch in Colorado. That was supposed "to get things fixed up," I suggested. Our two oldest children stayed with my mother and the twins stayed with her parents during that week long vacation in 1975.

Constructed in the 1950's, the ranch was an elaborate and beautiful series of buildings carved out of the Rocky Mountains. The main building was a massive semi circle of natural stone blending into the landscape. It housed the owners, the staff that served food and attended to other needs around the clock, and twenty or so couples. Behind it were several barns and stables made of gray wood that looked aged but not raggedy. The remainder of the crew, including the ranch hands, slept in various one story bunk houses of similar design.

If felt like a holiday right out of the movies. The quality of air that high in the mountains was concentrated, making it difficult to adjust to breathing at times. But it was so beautiful and surreal. On some mornings we looked down on the clouds.

Walking up hills on the nature trails was particularly challenging. and the first afternoon we elected to take a guided tour on horses. A dozen or so of us stood around wide-eyed and mildly startled as these strong, majestic animals whinnied, stomped, and stared. Having been drinking already that day, I was feeling a little snappy.

The ranch hand guiding that particular tour stood about six feet tall with thick, dark-brown hair. Though slender, his tanned skin was well toned and the muscles of his back and arms sturdy. He smiled a lot and winked at the ladies. I didn't like him.

He asked us "Okay, who here has ridden a horse before?"

The combination of beer induced grandiosity, and low self-esteem prevented me from telling the truth. It prevented me from saying "The closest I've ever come to a horse was the time I was nine and my grandpa took me to the circus." Instead, I felt my arm raise by some mysterious force as my hand waved and fingers signaled for attention. "I have," I lied, confidently proclaiming to be quite at home on the top of a horse. Nothing could have been further from the truth.

Big mouth me. Suddenly I'm a rodeo rider, saddled up on a gelded stallion.

So the ranch hand helped everyone mount and we rode for a while before reaching our first mountain pass. Jesus, was it a pass. I was one scared mother fucker looking over the top of that hill and realizing the horse would have to walk with deliberate concentration, cautiously placing one hoof in front of the other. "There is nothing to fear," soothed the sickening Elvis-like voice of the reassuring ranch hand. "These horses have done this many, many times, and they don't want to die either." He made eye contact with the ladies and rode up beside them to make sure they were "secure" in their western saddles. "Now just press your feet into the stirrup and hold on to the horn ma'am. Keep one hand on the reins if you can. You'll be fine." He paid far too much attention to my wife. The wife I was in Colorado with on our first vacation making a last-ditch effort to save my sinking marriage.

Having received no guidance as a self-proclaimed expert rider, I found myself leaning way forward and then way back, tightening every ligament, tendon, and joint in my body in an effort to hang on. The horse I rode appeared shrewd, so I settled in.

After a while I let myself get a little too relaxed. The stallion didn't like that and gave a kick from the rear as if to say "Pay attention or you'll be lying a few miles down at the bottom of that canyon." I probably had the only suicidal horse in the bunch. I tensed up and remained so for the rest of the day.

At the top of a pass about half way through the trail, my suicidal--or perhaps, homicidal--horse decided to take off at about a gazillion miles an hour and gallop across the pasture. My legs flailed haphazardly, looking much like a pair of too weak wings flapping low and quick on a clumsy duck. My arms clambered to get a firm grasp on the heedless reins. My had jerked in abrupt and darting movements atop my jelly-like neck. I lost total control over my destiny.

The stallion stopped just short of the path that lead straight down the side of the mountain.

Feeling completely humiliated, I tried to regain some composure. My face was still red and body trembling when the rest of the party caught up. Leading and smiling broadly, the ranch hand said "I thought you knew how to ride a horse Mr. Hammer" and cocked his cowboy hat-wearing head.

Acting as if I had commanded the stallion to gallop off at a gazillion miles an hour, I said "I do" quite assuredly. Right then I should have gotten off that son of a bitch. I was scared shitless. But no--I got to be Mr. Big Deal. Besides, I hate this ranch hand with the rich voice and twinkling eyes.

"Really?" he asked with delight. "Well, if you'd have just pulled back on the reins hard enough, the horse would have stopped running."

At that point, I was profoundly embarrassed and exceptionally perplexed. I was drunk when that nature tour began and I took a beer or two--or five--along with me. I started to cop an attitude with this guy. "Yeah, okay. Whatever you say big shot," I muttered, refusing to make eye contact with him and guiding my horse toward the slope of the hill. Suddenly this fucking horse turned around and bit me on the leg. HARD.

I started screaming and the ranch hand commanded "Kick him! Kick him!" Eventually I did and the horse let go of my leg. Then he said "If you get down off the horse and punch him in the face, he'll know who's boss" and guffawed, slapping himself on the thigh. I got it in my drunken and ill-functioning brain that the ranch hand instructed the horse to bite me through a series of gestures and head nods. I was one pissed off mother fucker.

The rest of the day is was one of the worst of my life. What could have been a beautiful trip through the mountains, full of the wondrous gifts and unique scenery, compliments of Mother Nature, was instead ruined by my alcoholism and my attitude. I spent the remainder of that afternoon fearful that at any given moment that stallion would splatter me against the side of a canyon wall.

Upon returning to our room, my first move was to drink half a fifth of bourbon chased by a beer within twenty minutes. Each passing swallow nourished the delusion that I was set up by that asshole ranch hand to look like an idiot in front of all those ladies, all those people. I grew angrier and angrier. "That smart-ass son of a bitch," I thought. "He made me look stupid so he would look cool. He spent all afternoon riding beside the women and patting their horses. He didn't do that with the men's horses. I wish he'd have told my horse something before it nearly killed me."

So I inhaled the bourbon and peeked out the window just in time to observe Mr. Big Shot ranch hand at the pool making the rounds with women. That included my wife who was sporting her new swim suit. I saw few husbands. Mr. ranch hand in his tight swim wear was strutting barefoot table to table making friendly with the wives while his package was hanging out and bouncing around all over the place. His big smiling face was sipping from his beer can and I decided I wanted to kill that son of a bitch. As a matter of fact, I was going to drown him.

As he made his way over to the diving board where my wife sat, I darted from my room and took off running about nine hundred miles an hour over the fifty or so feet that protected him from me. They were conversing as my fucked-up mind was thinking all the wrong things and I lunged through the air, inhaling as fully as I could, and plunged him into the pool and under the water.

My only thought was to make his big smile disappear under the water while bracing myself on the underside of the diving board so I could stay surfaced for air. That is exactly what I did.

Bubbles began to emanate as he must now exhale what little breath he was able to reserve without any warning. At the very last possible moment, and for no reason I can identify, I released him. To this day I thank The Universe for that. He popped to the surface, gasping for air. Too many more seconds would have been too many more seconds.

I swam to the edge of the pool and lifted myself out silently. I have no idea how anyone reacted. I don't remember looking. Besides the bubbles and his gasp for air I don't recall a sound.

I returned to my room, finished what little was left in the bottom of the bottle, got my 38 snub nose revolver out of my suitcase, and stuck it in my pocket. I sat outside on a patio chair with an umbrella over me for some time. Nobody said a thing. I barely remember the rest of the afternoon.

Somehow I talked the owners of the place into lending me a vehicle the following morning. I told Julie, "I don't care if I don't see another horse the rest of vacation. My ass hurts. My thighs hurt." My pride hurt. I said, "I'll be back in a few hours. Don't worry about me." I rode down into Denver and bought six bottles of bourbon. One for each of the remaining days we would spend at the ranch.

I walked around the rest of that week with a big chip on my shoulder, a bottle of bourbon in my hand, and a gun in my pants in case that ranch hand decided to sniper my ass when I least expected him.

That was my first vacation. What a fucked up mess.

ANGEL DUST

My two oldest children were twelve and eleven the night I was working the midnight shift and pulled into the station to find their mother, my soon to be ex-wife, had pulled in immediately and precariously close behind me. I parked my car as usual and walked to her vehicle hoping this meeting was coincidental and I could get away with some small talk.

"Hey, who's home with the kids?" I asked, after some congenial hellos. I glanced at the blue numbers on the clock in her car. *What's going on? Why are you here?*

Looking only mildly startled she began going on about how someone was lurking around the house and she was afraid he was trying to break in. I had just recently chased some guy off the porch and although my gut didn't believe her my brain kept racing *"The kids are home alone."*

"I'll follow you home." Keying into the cruiser I said urgently "C'mon! Now! The kids are home alone." A little embarrassed by some of her previous antics, I didn't tell anyone at the station I was going in the event this proved to be a trick.

Once at the home where we had once lived as a family, I parked and got out my flash light. There were no pry marks, no foot prints, no bent bushes, nothing to indicate anyone had tried to break in as I walked around the entire house. I stepped inside to secure all the doors and windows to discover the living room lit up by dozens of candles. It felt eerie and discomforting.

"What are you doing?" I asked Julie, who sat on the couch quite obviously rolling a joint.

"Rolling a joint," she said calmly.

My addiction kicked in. Not trusting her motives for bringing me here but not wanting to turn down a free buzz either, I ignored my instincts. I sat down and smoked it with her.

The white smoke rising from three candles on the coffee table danced, transforming into three faces. They mouthed soundless songs and spoke silent words. I quickly realized she laced the joint with something. But it was too late. I'd already smoked it.

"What the hell is in this joint?" I demanded.

"PCP," she said coolly. "Angel dust." She smiled like the Cheshire cat.

Angel dust and I had met before. We would also have a relationship later on . . . but it was not always a good experience. However, I would not have smoked PCP and gone to work as a cop at that point in my career for Christ's sake. And I was certainly not up for what was about to happen.

Unexpectedly and suddenly, a deranged, contorted, deep, unfamiliar voice came out of my estranged wife's mouth. It said "I am the Lord thy God. You need to be forgiven for your sins and must kneel down in front of me. I am God so only I can forgive your sins."

A solid wave of cold rushed through my body. I remembered the time she told me "One of these nights I am going to stab you to death in your sleep." Here it was, only I wasn't sleeping.

With my portable radio in my hand I attempted a response which came out rather shaky. "What the hell is the matter with you?" My nerves were trembling from the inside out.

"Kneel and beg for forgiveness," she pointed near the stairway.

"You're fucking nuts, that's what you are. Whatever the hell is in your mind right now is crazier than fuck! You're not thinking right." I stood up and moved cautiously towards the kitchen to put some distance between us. *What if I have to shoot her?* I thought. Leaving the house was not an option as all four of my children slept upstairs.

Further enraged, her deep voice grew angrier, louder, more demanding of submission.

Just then, my oldest son came down the stairs looking sleepy and scared. Julie commanded him in that demonic voice "Saint Thomas, I order you to kill the devil. That man is the devil and you must kill him."

He stuttered "I c-c-c-can't do that."

My oldest daughter came down the stairs immediately behind him. "What's wrong? What's going on? What's going on?!!" she screamed, insisting on an answer.

Julie was rambling almost unintelligibly by then and the extra chaos diverted her long enough for me to usher them onto the back porch. I heard the twins rustling as the nightmare downstairs got louder and scarier. "Run to your grandparents'," I instructed the oldest two, as my parents at that time lived only two blocks down the street. "Stay there." That was all I had time to say. I needed to get back inside to the younger children, who were only seven.

But in the few short seconds it took me to get back to the door she had slammed and locked it with the security locks I had put on myself when I moved out. I had to call for back-up.

"I need some help down here. Something is terribly wrong." Aware that others besides those in law enforcement may be listening, I gave out as much information as I could over my radio without divulging the insanity occurring in my former home. The next several minutes were the longest of my life. While anxiously awaiting for back-up to arrive, I kept my eyes glued to the doors and windows praying that at any moment the twins would come running out or give me some sign they were safe.

When the other officers arrived I told them what was going on while leaving out the part about Julie and I smoking a joint laced with PCP. The situation had sobered me up to a functional level; I found that if I stayed focused on getting my kids out of that house alive I could perceive and communicate rather sensibly. Anything sounding irrational could be adequately explained by nerves.

It was almost an hour after this horrific night began that Officer Dettmer, a very trustworthy friend, made the decision to break down the door. Julie did not respond to any attempts to resolve the situation, including the use of a bull horn. Once inside the house, he then had to break down her bedroom door. He later said he found my children sitting on either side of their mother on the bed looking terrified and confused.

Two other officers removed Julie from the bedroom. She had become rather docile as she started to come down from her high and was placed at Toledo State Mental Hospital.

The twins told officer Dettmer that they had been in the utility room, unsure of where to hide, when "all the noise started outside." My youngest daughter said they were forced to kneel down on their knees and my youngest son told him "Mom said it may be necessary to sacrifice us. What does that mean?"

"It's okay now. You're going to be fine. You're safe and your mommy is going someplace they can help her get better. Your daddy is right outside." Officer Dettmer didn't know what else to say.

Nothing was ever the same after that. I never had another direct conversation with Julie again.

LETTER

Dear Bill,

I have returned to Ohio. I came home five days ago.

Raye was a pirate for Halloween. Samantha was a vampire. Susan dressed as a cowgirl for the parade and then had to work.

Jim missed you. I spent about an hour on the phone with Friday night. He told me that you were, with me, the man you had always wanted to be. At times, I struggle to separate the only you I ever knew from the you some of your relatives remember.

What I knew was the man who walked on the outside of me down the sidewalk, nearest the street, so he would be the one hit should a car jump the curb . . . the man who rubbed lotion on my legs every Saturday morning after my bath . . . the man who brought me flowers every anniversary and Valentine's Day.

I never knew the man who came home so drunk one night he never made it inside the house and awoke the next morning to find himself frozen to the picnic table . . . the man who had to unzip he jeans and slide out of them so he could go inside . . . the man who said "So many times I thought about how I should be at home with my family, not waking up in strange places with no recollection of how I got there."

I think about the first AA meeting you told me about going to after you detoxed yourself at home in 1990. How a friend, seeing you shake violently while trying to hold a cup of coffee whispered in your ear "You never have to feel this way again," and how that sentence would be one of many that helped save your life. One that ensured you would find your way to me to help me save mine.

I wanted you to stay alive a little longer. I wanted to love you some more.

Where do I belong now Bill? You were my home and my home died.

How long will I have to tell you goodbye? When will it feel like you haven't just pulled out of the garage? As if I can't see your tail lights dimming as you drive down the street? Like if I strain my calves and will my heart to pump all the blood I have in me it will allow me to catch up to you, scream your name, make you see me in the rearview mirror, force you pull over so I can collapse into your embrace and hear you say "I'll be right back, baby. I'll be right back."

How long Bill? How long?

The sky is soft blue today. It is the first day of November. There is a slight wind and a few fluffy clouds. Cars start and stop on the street. This picture would look okay if you were in it.

I miss you.

Love, your adoring wife- Jenn

PURPLE

Bill painted my bedroom purple for me. Two walls a deep, rich plum like a beautiful warm cobbler. The other two a soft feathery lilac, like the color of a title on a romance novel. I slept there, surrounded on all sides by the notion that I'm swinging gently in the knowing hammock of an eternal dusk.

In October of 1968 Bill enjoyed such a sunset. It was his first night as a police officer. The hour before he went on duty he put on his new pressed uniform and sat in the backyard on his children's swing set watching the sky pull on her velvety robe, fuzzy and easily bruised, like a violet. He described the joy in his heart as he waited to get started. "I like people," he explained. "I've always liked people. There was just a long period of time when I didn't like me."

I always wished I could time travel when he said things like this. I would have walked right up to him on that slide, told him how proud I am of him, what a good man he will become, beg him not to do some of the things he would eventually do.

Early in his career, Bill responded to one of many fire calls. In an effort to survive, two little boys, ages four and five had attempted to escape the hot flames ravaging their home by huddling in various rooms throughout the house. They died of smoke inhalation. A firefighter had handed one of those precious little lifeless bodies to Bill. "He just looked like he was sleeping. I wrapped him up in a sheet. I wanted to cry. I needed to forget that and I chose to drink. I had nightmares about it for years. It never dawned on me that there were other ways to go on. I did not deal with these enormous feelings until I got sober." Bill did not deal with most of his feelings until he got sober.

Bill had some periods of sobriety over the years. A year and a half here. Twenty two months there. Inevitably, something would overcome him. He would return to drinking, fuck up some more, feel more ashamed of himself, and then drink to deal with that.

The man who sat in his backyard that first night as a cop imagining the safe, happy life he would provide for his family disappeared slowly like the sun behind clouds. His hopes about the kind of father and husband he would be plunged deeper into his core, inaccessible, as if he had been stabbed by a sharp sword determined to rob him of his blood, his entire reason for being on the planet. And for a long time, it succeeded.

Bill was not innately equipped to handle this much human frailty. My husband was a haunted man. Fragility only made his already struggling sense of finite power to rescue more impotent. He was vigilantly aware of his limitations and he hated them. He hated them until he hated himself. And he hated himself until eventually, he hated everyone who cared about him. "I don't believe I hit a bottom" he had observed about his addiction. "I believe I wallowed around in it for years. I drank and drugged for twenty five years. My behavior was reprehensible."

If Bill's God had told him that branding the word "alcoholic" on his forehead would have freed him years ago of the bondage of that disease, my husband would have done it.

If Bill's God had told me that I could have spared him every ounce of pain that disease caused himself and others by saying just the right words to him the night I stepped off the time machine as the sky turned purple, even if it meant having never met Bill as a result, I would have done that, too.

FRED SANDUSKY

It's shortly after 8:30 on a sultry Monday evening as I drive around the Seneca County country side absorbing the pink of the setting sun in the sky which always looks closer to the ground in summertime. My arm flies out the open window of my foamy green mini-van despite the heavy heat of the wind rushing over me.

I could go home but I feel born again this moment and birth always requires new exposure to bright lights, unmuffled sounds, and all things not too familiar. So I will drive for a time, watching and listening.

A client of my colleague gave a lead tonight; she is thirty three months free from slavery. Free from crack cocaine and alcohol and trouble they inevitably invite. She told the story of running home after school as a child, trying to hide from the girl who beat her up daily. Her older sister tired of seeing her run and eventually told her "You gotta fight that girl or you gotta fight me!" So she stopped running, started fighting for herself, and stopped feeling so afraid all the time. That is what addiction is like. Sooner or later, you've got to stop running.

During her closing she thanked several of the forty or so people in the room. Unexpectedly, she said "there is somebody here tonight who is very special to me. He was here ten years ago when I first came in to the program and I remember him shaking my hand, hugging me, and telling me it was going to be all right." She was talking to me.

She reminded me that this Thursday, July 6, 2000, it will have been ten years since I began my life over. In three days I will have been clean and sober for a decade. This moment feels bigger to me than any moment which has come and gone before. She makes me remember.

I remember a man, present since childhood, who played an integral role in the decisions I made in adulthood, including the one to get sober. His name was Fred Sandusky.

For my ninth birthday Frank gave me an erector set; it was the best one on the market at the time. It was my very own mini-construction site neatly compacted in a little metal box, complete with a steam shovel, little buildings . . . I played with it in conjunction with my Lincoln logs and my cowboys and Indians set. The gift gave me a sense of mastery. I could put things together and tear them apart, too. I would do a little of both through the journey that would become my life.

Perhaps the little erector set influenced my choice to work in construction during the years between working as a police officer and becoming a counselor. Now that I think about it, Fred inspired many of my career decisions. After getting sober himself, he went on to become a probation officer in Tiffin, helping adolescent offenders. After getting sober myself, I went on to become a Chemical Dependency Counselor, originally co-facilitating an adolescent Intensive Outpatient Program. But it was at a carnival in the summer of 1968 I decided to become a police officer.

My oldest son and daughter walked on either side of me, licking cotton candy and candy apple off their faces when I heard Fred say "Hey Bill! How are you? Come on over here a second, we were just talking about you." A handsome man, standing at least six feet two inches and weighing a sturdy and solid 200 pounds, Fred Sandusky stood next to his fellow officer, both fully uniformed, looking mysterious, yet orderly. He introduced me to Officer Smith, who had black hair and sculptured features and gave me a strong, confidant hand shake and smiled warmly. His uniform looked stately against his dark complexion. Their presence seemed inviting and important. I wanted what they had.

"We're going to be having a test for police officers coming up. Why don't you apply? Why don't you join us Bill? I was just telling him about you," Fred said, nodding his head toward Officer Smith. I didn't need coerced. I'd wanted my whole life to feel important. Like what I did mattered, made a difference to someone, somewhere. I wanted to be one of the good guys. And Fred Sandusky, friend to my father, godfather to me, thought I would be a good police officer.

"I think I will, Fred." I decided without further pondering to do just that.

At about the same time the Seneca County Sherriff's department was holding a test for deputies which I also took. I passed both tests and impatiently waited for either opportunity to pan out though I very much wanted to stay local. But the sheriff's office called first. Though excited, the memory of standing in the presence of Officer Smith and Officer Sandusky at that carnival relived itself frequently in my mind. I had watched as passersby looked suspiciously from the corner of their eye, wondering what we talked about. The aura of protection, power, honor, and prestige dense around us the way a fog hovers over a fertile valley. I wanted to be a cop for all the right reasons . . . and some of the wrong ones. In my early naiveté, I assumed all cops became cops this way.

I made a visit to Chief James Mikes. Having worked with my father, he was a family friend and told me confidentially to "Hang in there. You are in the top three candidates and I expect you will be offered a job soon. But the civil service commission has to make the announcement."

After another long week of waiting, I made another trip. This time down to his house; he told me the same thing.

Eventually, the waiting paid off and the announcement was made that I would be appointed to the Fostoria Police Department the same shift as Captain Fred. I was elated. Captain Fred was a well-liked man whose mere presence commanded respect. He had worked for the department for about twenty years. There was just that one tiny rumor . . . that he had a bit of a drinking problem.

The night I accepted the offer I ventured into the back yard and sat on my children's swing set, gazing at the stars in the clear and configured heavenly display of constellations. I remember thinking that I had made something of myself. I did something right. I would be a police officer. I would provide for my family all the while serving my community working in a respectable profession which made good use of my skills and talents.

I don't remember when that stopped making sense. But I often wish it wouldn't have.

After I worked my first week or so, Captain Fred invited me down to his house for a drink with the understanding we would go out later. His second wife, a kind and pretty woman twenty years his junior, was at work. He pulled a bottle of Kessler's Whiskey from the cupboard and set it in front of us. Next he retrieved two 10 ounces glasses and proceeded to pour about nine and three fourth ounces of the whiskey into his glass and looked at me. I held up my index finger and my thumb about two fingers width indicating this was all the whiskey I wanted. He retrieved a bottle of 7-up, filling my glass with soda and splashing it across the top of his.

Fred was already shaking as he brought the "mixed drink" to his lips and drank it in about two swallows. He became very talkative as he poured a second drink identical to his first and decided he was taking me down to The Manhattan to celebrate my new career. Typically, whiskey gave me a horrendous hangover, made me do things I regretted, and burnt my throat. I sipped mine that night. Kessler's and I would become much closer later.

As we descended the stairs off the small front porch of the old duplex I watched as Fred, who made a clumsy attempt to grab for the side rail, flopped over backwards into the hedgerow.

He let out quite a grunt, sounding like "kuhoo" but made no attempt to get up. At this exact time his wife arrived home.

She approached the porch looking disgusted but was considerably less vocal than I anticipated. It was as though this was not the first time she had seen her husband in such a condition. Between the two of us we were able to get him out of the bushes and back up to their apartment. "Thanks." she said politely, "he'll sleep it off." I went home.

Now that I think about it, I never did drink at a bar with Captain Fred. He never made it that far.

THE RIOT I CAUSED

It wasn't all bad--the things I did in my life as a cop, or as a drunk for that matter. At times, the best moments of my life have occurred on my worst days. Other times, the worst moments of my life have occurred on days which had the best potential. I supposed this is true for most people.

After a seven day work rotation on a steaming Friday one August, my second wife and I planned to meet my buddy and his wife in New Riegle for some ribs and drinks. This guy had volunteered for three tours in Viet Nam and lived his life in constant anticipation of the next great battle. He was crazy, and I often got myself into some trouble with him.

I anticipated the next four days off, and subsequent partying, the way many men may look forward to a cruise on the Caribbean with their spouse or a fishing trip with their lifelong friends. It was like a vacation; a full mind and body shut down. My spouse was the liquid in the bottle. I'd already had about ten beers when we began driving the ten or so miles back to Fostoria, where we intended to make the rounds at the pubs.

Suddenly, the vehicle immediately in front of us veered off the right side of the road and into the ditch. There was no warning. As we slowed, it came flying out of the ditch, twisting and rolling in the air and landing upside down in a culvert full of water, the way a diver would torpedo into a pool after leaping off the board.

Emerging from the tangled wreck, a frantic and hysterical woman climbed the grassy hill flailing her arms and screaming, "My baby's in there! My baby's in there! Help, help, PLEASE somebody help, please . . . my baby . . ."

I took off running.

Fortunately, the baby's tiny little body was easy to locate. Unfortunately, she was lifeless. I placed her face down on my arm to expel what water I could before beginning CPR. Then, turning her back over, I breathed a short puff of air into her lungs. She choked immediately and began breathing on her own. I hadn't expected her to respond so quickly; my body rushed with warmth. My spirit became inflated and consumed with a triumph which felt both exclusive and overwhelming. The sound around me rippled in circles of silence. The air paused calm and still. The faces on the people in my surrounding smiled slow and permanent. The mystery of life and death appeared tangible, yet transparent, and now possible to defy. For a split second, the universe made perfect sense.

Then the second was gone. I heard the sirens and saw the men running towards me. They whisked the baby from my cradled and protective arms. These arms--this mouth, this breath which had just restored her life. The baby and her mother disappeared into the back of the ambulance. They would both live. For now. But many people would die around them. Maybe tonight in the room next to theirs. And the universe would feel so random again.

We went to a crowded bar on the South end. I ordered some shots and was plenty liquored up when I recognized a guy who I'd let put his hands on me a couple weeks ago on a domestic violence call. Instantly my angry blood coursed through my veins with an intense desire for revenge. Hitting women, pushing police officers, who did this son-of-a-bitch think he was? How dare he embarrass me like that! How could I have let him? I had to make this make sense, even the score. Now.

So I "accidentally" pushed my second wife, Rhonda, into him and raised my voice, "What the hell do you think you're doing touching my wife?" Rhonda, startled and wide-eyed like a deer caught in head lights, jumped out of the way as this man and I began a shoving match. Then I made what was to prove to be the biggest mistake of the evening.

"Let's step outside." I invited him, pointing towards the street through the open door.

About one hundred or so patrons, an almost even mix of black and white drunk people, followed us out. He opened his car door in the parking lot and retrieved a gun. Things were happening too quickly. A sane person would have taken cover, begun apologizing, run even. Not me. I looked at my friend who was always better armed than an on duty police officer. He carried a 9 MM in a shoulder holster, a 45 caliber tucked into his waistband, a derringer in his pocket somewhere, and a little 22 caliber hand gun already gripped in his palm. He'd found his next battle. I carried a 38 caliber snub nose.

I had made life and death decisions on that Friday night in August. I had that kind of control, that kind of power. I had breathed into a small body and made her choke with life.

We started towards him. Apparently he was the saner man that night--he DID run. He ran fast off into the night.

I felt robbed, cheated of my chance to redeem myself. He had put his hands on me in front of his wife and another officer and I had done nothing. And now he was running.

In a fiery moment of frustration and rage I kicked the glass out of the passenger side window of his car. The shattering of the glass sounded concrete and definite. My friend hopped up and down on top of the car until it touched the seats. The screeching of the roof sounded complete and permanent. I ran around the car, denting his hub caps and breaking his head lights with my angry, self-righteous, wounded and wounding, hurt and hurting, pained and paining kicks.

Then I heard "What's going on here Bill?" from a cruiser which had recently arrived.

"Oh nothing," I answered all nonchalantly, "Everything is under control here."

He left.

The man who had fled a few minutes before now returned, bringing with him somewhere between twenty and thirty of his friends. The name calling started. Niggers. Crackers. The whole gamut. Small groups of people screaming at each other, swinging at each other over something they knew nothing about.

All because I had saved a baby's life earlier, and in the moments after realized she could have died if I had been more intoxicated, if our car hadn't been behind theirs, if the water had been deeper, if she'd flown out of the car and been more difficult to retrieve, if her mother had been too shocked to tell us she was in the car . . . if . . . if . . . if . . .

I looked over towards my friend and witnessed the man I had shoved my wife into, starting all this, running towards him. I screamed out a warning just in time for my friend to swing his right fist into the man's jaw. I heard it break. His body splatted on the asphalt the way batter lands in a frying pan. By now the police were arriving. More than one hundred people were involved in some form or fashion. The two groups of people got broken up with the whites standing on one side of the mess and the blacks on the other. The cops stood in the middle, dividing them. We were begging the police to leave and "Let street justice prevail." This was about justice after all, wasn't it? About things that are right and things that are wrong? About life and death? About honor and disgrace? Wasn't it? Wasn't it?

Someone was able to get me in the darkness and confusion. A sudden, hard push sent me through the plate glass window of a store front across the street where the riot had moved out of the parking lot. No sooner had I crashed through than Denny Shoreman, a fellow officer, grabbed the front of my shirt and jerked me from the window, just in time to hear the crash of the remaining top half land like a guillotine. It would have sliced me in half.

So someone saved my life that Friday night in August, too.

I was placed under arrest for disorderly conduct and told to report to the police department, which was less than a block away around the corner. They added the charge to my file and suspended me for fifteen days without pay. Civil court instructed me to pay half of the damages to the man whose jaw was wired shut for an unusually lengthy time. Eventually, I paid about half of what I was ordered to and used the suspension to get drunk and blame everyone else for what I had done.

I don't know if saving that baby's life on the day I started a race riot was one of my best moments on one of my worst days, or if starting a race riot on the day I saved a baby's life was one of my worst moments on one of my best days. Sometimes I wish I did.

"CALL ME GOD"

While cruising the South end of town one warm summer afternoon in the late 1970's I received the call that a six foot five inch tall African American man was marching down the middle of Lytle Street in Army fatigues. A four lane highway which runs the center of the town, Lytle Street was jammed with stopped traffic and curious onlookers. I parked the cruiser in front of The Lunch Box and got out, against my better judgment, as backup had not yet arrived. They were still several blocks away, I was informed via radio.

Slowly and thoughtfully I approached the marching man. "Sir, may I speak with you?" There was no response, so I took another step and asked again without raising my voice. "Sir, may I speak with you?"

Suddenly the subject halted, made a perfect about face, and called out "Are you talking to me boy? If you are, call me General Eisenhower," as he saluted me.

"Yes sir, General Eisenhower," I responded. "Sir, may I speak with you?"

General Eisenhower ignored my request, made another about face, and continued marching.

I called out to him again. The general stopped and made yet another about face, staring at me boldly.

His voice thickened. "Are you talking to me boy? If you are, you can call me God."

My stomach churned; the churn you get when you're sent to your room as a kid to "think about what you've done" and you know the worst is yet to come. General Eisenhower I could have handled—perhaps--but God? What do I say to him . . . and without back up?

"God, I need to speak to you," I tried.

He simply marched away.

I heard the sirens from the back up unit closing in as I cautiously followed him down the center of the four lane highway. Screeching to a halt, the officers hopped out of their cruiser and came racing to my side. Just then, the man stepped out of configuration and took a swing at me with his enormous fist. Thinking I was outside of striking distance, I jumped back quickly but narrowly and took quite a punch to my ribs. Hugging my rib cage, I lost balance and my knees buckled, hitting the hard pavement.

Both back up officers struggled with the suspect and managed to wrestle him to the concrete where he was now crawling to the curb. He attempted to regain his posture as one officer slammed his head into the curb and the other sprayed mace in his face. They managed to get him handcuffed in his confusion.

Shaking his head violently, tears from his eyes and snot from his nose flying everywhere, he was aided to his feet and looked at me sorrowfully. "Do you have a cigarette?" he asked. I obliged.

His name was Winston and he had walked out of a VA hospital in Brecksville, a suburb of Cleveland. A highly decorated hero in the Korean War, Winston explained that he had a difficult time distinguishing between current reality and previous memory while having flashbacks and today had been a particularly bad one. We call this PTSD today. Winston and I ate lunch together later that afternoon and I listened as he spoke of his experiences.

His reward for defending his country was to live with a mental condition which robbed him of his life. Perhaps forever. He wore the face of a man who was promised a huge raise and promotion after a job well done and finished the job only to find he'd been tricked. The face of a man who'd weighed carefully his words and balanced every earnest deed his entire life to arrive at the pearly gates and discover there was no Heaven. The face of a man who'd farmed the land as a sharecropper only to find himself at the end of twenty years served and realize the recently deceased land owner left the property to his oldest son in his will. He wore the face of a man who had been cheated. And there was no way to get it back.

He made me sad.

The ache in my ribs felt insignificant.

THE NAKED MAN

Officer Dettmer and I were at Candy Land Restaurant eating breakfast at the end of our shift one morning the late 1970's when the portable radio came alive with one of the strangest reports I'd ever heard.

Captain Kinkler, who was seriously wounded several years earlier after surviving a stab to the head, announced over the airways that a young naked man had just passed down the center of Main Street. The location he gave was four blocks south of the restaurant where we shoved our last bits of toast and egg in our mouths and headed for the door. Captain Kinkler advised us to "approach him with extreme caution."

The front window in Candy Land gave us an unobstructed view of Main Street. Within seconds of receiving the call we observed, sure as shit, stark ass naked, a man marching down the middle of the street. Officer Dettmer and I ran for the cruiser.

At an intersection, the naked man turned onto a side street but remained marching directly down the center. Three other cruisers joined us, including Captain Kinkler. Two cruisers drove along on either side of him, one behind him, and I drove in front of him. We had him boxed in and attempted to coral him near the sidewalk. This plan failed miserably as the naked man simply stepped onto the hood of my cruiser, never missing a beat.

However, he lost his footing on the slippery surface and slid on his hands and knees backwards into a big plate glass window of a local business, a pet store called "Tropical Cove," shattering it so suddenly I don't remember the sound. A huge shard of glass remained at the top of the frame and clung for just a second before gravity pulled it down. Luckily he hadn't gone head first because it fell, slicing a huge chunk of his ass off when it landed, breaking the silence.

I again heard the familiar crackle on the cruiser radio and the crunch of the gritty glass crashing on the side walk and bits scattering and scraping across the hood of the car.

As if on fast forward, the naked main regained his balance, jumped off the cruiser, and ran off like a jack rabbit through the store's corner parking lot, chunk of ass missing, trailing blood and all. The first building he reached was the Catholic Church and he attempted to enter through a locked side door. Although I would not have been able to penetrate the thick but small stained-glass window beside it with my night stick, he simply balled up his fist and punched a hole through it, reached in, and unlocked the door.

Fortunately the church was empty due to a special holiday which had altered the schedule. Normally, it would have been filled with as many as twenty nuns and one hundred or so parishioners at that time.

"Crucify me! Crucify me! Crucify me!" He yelled repeatedly from upon the altar area where he stood with his arms raised and his ass bleeding on the pure white altar cloth.

I looked at Officer Dettmer. "Holy shit, what's he on? He thinks he's Jesus Christ."

We decided to pull him down from the altar first, get him on the ground, and then cuff him once he was on the floor. Bad plan for a man who, as we would find out later, was taking a very bad PCP trip and was as strong as he believed himself to be. Though we successfully pulled him down, holding him down proved to be virtually impossible. Naked man, aka Jesus Christ on Angel Dust, threw off a 270 pound officer with his right arm alone and landed a 240 pound man on his back with a toss from his left. Three officers held his legs down while he proceeded to scream only "Crucify me!" We were unable to immobilize him; panic was about to set in.

As I reached for his arm his muscles tensed. Unexpectedly and without thinking I said as naturally as could be, "Jesus Christ, hold still, we can't get the nails in if you won't hold still." He relaxed.

Just as the ambulance arrived and the stretcher was wheeled in we finished cuffing his arms and legs behind him. He was delivered safely to the ER and I spoke with him several hours later after he'd come down from his PCP trip. Though only acquaintances, I'd known his family and they were extremely embarrassed by his behavior that day.

"What did I do?" he asked me.

He didn't flinch once as I told him, as though some vague and remote corner of his mind already knew. Like it was the retelling of a movie he watched parts of while falling in and out of sleep and needed someone else to fill in the missing pieces and confirm that what he remembered had not been a dream. He helped me by giving information which enabled the police department to confiscate this particularly dangerous batch of Angel dust from our community.

Years later I ran into the naked man, who was now fully clothed at a bar I frequented. Over several drinks we conversed briefly. It was mostly small talk and local gossip. Clearly, something irreversible happened to him the morning he took that bad PCP trip, marching around town naked, losing a chunk of his ass, and begging to be crucified like Jesus Christ. His thinking was illogical and scattered. His conversation, at times, nonsense.

He was never again the same bright young man full of a future and potential. He was never again the man he had been only several hours before taking a drug that landed him bleeding and begging to be killed in a church one early morning in the late 1970's.

"EAT YOUR DRIVER'S LICENSE"

By 1978 I was secretly smoking marijuana daily during my shift. A couple of pre-rolled joints, I found, fit nicely tucked into the front pocket of my uniform. The habit seemed an easier one to hide. While my friends, family, and fellow officers knew I drank, no one knew I also smoked pot while on duty. Stan was no exception.

A graduate of Bowling Green State University, Stan moved to Fostoria when he took a job with The Fostoria Review times as a photo-journalist. He lived in a duplex owned by my friend Jake, who occupied the other half. In addition to seeing him there, I often stumbled upon him taking photographs at the scene of an accident. In a way, our professions kind of drew us together, the tool of my trade being a service revolver and his a camera. I liked Stan immediately. As our friendship blossomed, he accompanied me on many occasions when I worked midnights and my primary responsibility was to drive the streets of Fostoria responding to calls.

Perhaps one of the most obnoxious events he ever witnessed while on one of these nightly cruises through town occurred in the summer of 1978. A swerving vehicle, which nearly struck several parked cars and then proceeded to jump a curb and run through the front yard of a residence, caught our attention. Despite the activation of both my lights, and briefly, my siren, the driver continued making his way haphazardly down the street. We followed him with lights flashing and the siren turned back on and blaring for several more minutes. Eventually, he pulled over. Stan, who by now knew the procedure, remained in the cruiser while I approached the driver to investigate.

Immediately, I recognized him as a city councilman. Also a manager in one of the local factories, he was a rather verbal presence at council meetings. Once a relatively svelte individual who fancied himself a ladies' man, he was now in his mid forties with a deteriorating physique.

This included the traditional beer belly. As an elected official whose job it was to represent his

constituents, he regarded himself, by route of some illogical sequence of thought, my boss. This

perturbed me greatly.

"Hhhhhhhhhammer!" slurred the drunken voice from the crack in the window he'd barely

rolled down. "Don't you know who am, I mean who am I, I mean, Fuck. YOU know what I

mean. I'll have your badge for this. You're an asshole. You son of a bitch . . ." He was sloppy

drunk and trailed off into some pompous rhetoric about his relative universal importance and my

own inferior status in the grand scheme of things.

I asked for his license, which in those days were still in paper. He fumbled through his

glove compartment and thrust a bunched up clump of paper in my hand. I decided to make him

get out of the car and perform some sobriety tests.

He responded by opening his car door and falling flat on his face.

Time for some pictures, I decided. I went back to the cruiser and asked Stan to follow me

with his camera. "Take some pictures of the important councilman," I suggested.

Stan's flash sporadically lit the scene as the drunken and very important, indeed super big

deal councilman, attempted repeatedly to rise. Each white light and subsequent failure to stand

resulted in grander verbal bantering by the councilman. I was stoned out of my mind. For the

most part, I recall thinking the entire event was rather humorous. Stan danced around shooting

him in a variety of compromising angles. I laughed.

"What the hell's goin' on?" He demanded. "You're an asshole Hammer." He was

oblivious. "I don't have to do jack shit for you- you're no p'lice officer. I'll have you fired. You

asshole- just like your father . . . no p'lice officer . . ."

That did it.

"He's going to eat his driver's license," I told Stan rather boldly and began rolling it into a small ball.

Ever the logical and rational thinker with the ability to reason through actions and connect them to their consequences, Stan advised against doing such a thing.

"Who will ever believe it? You're not going to say anything which makes it my word against his."

He was still unable to regain his footing and pleading for help to get up when I leaned over the councilman and shoved the license into his mouth with his next words. Like a vice, I placed one hand firmly under his jaw and the other on top of his head and held his mouth shut.

He called my father an asshole.

"If you ever want to get up, you WILL eat your driver's license," I informed him. After a brief struggle, he gulped.

I don't know if he was too humiliated or if it was that he was too drunk to register what had happened but he made no attempt to tell on me once we were at the station. He foolishly took the breathalyzer and blew close to the .3 range.

It was no excuse to make a man eat his driver's license. There was no excuse.

Until recently, I had completely forgotten I'd done this to a man who was quite possibly a soul sick as myself. A man whose only solace was found in a dark, thin bottle at the Knights of Columbus. A man who got really drunk and did things and said things he wished later he wouldn't have . . . just like me.

FIRST INPATIENT STAY

Fred Sandusky had been a police officer for about twenty years when I became one. His alcoholism had reached late stage with reverse tolerance. In 1970, the administration and city officials approached him with the option to go on medical leave and immediately retire as it was evident he could no longer function as an officer.

He struggled through eleven days of detox at Rosary Hall in Akron. Sister Ignatia, one of the early organizers of Alcoholics Anonymous in Cleveland, worked there at the time. There was no detox using Valium, Phenobarbital, Sodium Pentothal, in those days. The regimen was to reduce the alcohol intake and give some Paraldehyde either in the form of an enema or anal suppository to reduce the shakes and hope you make it. Every few hours, gradually reduced, Fred got a shot of whiskey and some humiliating injection of Paraldehyde up his ass over those eleven days. He made it.

After a few months Fred came back and he looked good. His eyes were no longer yellow. His hard, distended stomach was softer and smaller. He had some pink in his skin.

"The entire time I felt like my insides were going to blow apart, the pressure in my chest was awful. All I did was yearn for a drink. But here I am. I better do something about that." So he did.

Fred went over to Tiffin and got a job as a probation officer in Seneca County. His big hands wrapped around mine when we had the opportunity to meet. I knew how he felt about me when he gave me a hand shake. What an important symbol that became to me.

At the time, I was still a police officer in Fostoria and dealing with my own family problems. Fred became very active in Tiffin AA and mending some broken fences of his own. We saw each other sporadically and coincidentally over the next decade.

Then one night in 1980 I went into work drunk and picked up a bunch of warrants for some of the more dastardly people in town. I decided to hit the bars and arrest them- by myself. I stopped uptown at The Smokehouse and was informed by the bartender that a guy I was looking for had just slipped out the back door. *"I'm in no mood to go chasing this guy down the alley,"* I thought. *"Besides, it's just for a silly failure to appear."* Gary, the bartender, gestured to me that he was pouring me a glass of 7-up, with a couple shots of something clear in it, wink-wink. Taking a seat at the bar, it occurred to me that I was not out serving arrest warrants at all.

After several hours, several drinks, and several bars, I landed on the east side of town at a place called The Godfather, which traditionally served African American patrons. Suddenly, I recognized a guy who eluded me earlier and decided to arrest him. My opportunity to prove I was actually serving warrants, just like I'd said. However, we were both shit faced and it became apparent as the interaction escalated that I was going to require back up. Somebody called the station. Fortunately I had a good reputation and about half the bar assisted in preventing me from getting my ass kicked. My drink was still sitting on the bar when some of the younger officers arrived and made the actual arrest. I picked it up and proceeded to walk out the back door directly into the red and sweating face of Sergeant DeMans. "What are you drinking Bill?"

Despite the fact that I was very clearly intoxicated I lied "7-up."
"Give it to me," he ordered. Like a fool, I handed it to him gently instead of letting it 'slip' out of my hand. He smelled it. By this time I don't know how many shots of whatever were being mixed into my splash of 7-up. But, like Fred's drinks years before, there was significantly less soda.

"Report to the captain's office, immediately" he said without blinking.

I knew I was in T-R-O-U-B-L-E.

Panic set in. I parked the cruiser back at the station and walked into the captain's office, stood there for approximately ten seconds, walked through the door out which led into the hall way, exited through the back, got back into my car, and drove home. I had a few more drinks to ease my anticipation. No one contacted me that night.

Upon my arrival to work the following day I was summoned to Captain Kinkler's office. He told me the drink had been tested and alcohol had been found in its contents. I knew there was no method for immediate testing and responded with "I wonder how that got in there? Maybe I picked up the wrong drink as I was walking out." It didn't work.

"Bill, we know that you have been drinking heavily and you have some, oh, problems in your life."

And I did. Alcohol had already become more important than my second marriage.

He proposed I go for treatment.

What a relief! I wasn't going to lose my job. "I'll jump any hoop they want me to," I thought. And when it's all over with . . . I'll still be a cop.

"Okay" I said rather nonchalantly.

Fred, now well into his fifties with a decade of recovery behind him, sounded very encouraging over the phone. "Pack a toothbrush and toothpaste. They don't give you that stuff you know, you have to take it. You sleep in your own pajamas and all that." He volunteered to drive me up there. "Be ready in the morning. Early."

"Fred," I stammered, "I don't know if I can go that fast, I have…"

"I'll be there by 6:30. Be ready in the morning."

I was ready in the morning.

It was a fourteen day program. •I had no physical detox and resigned myself to using the time to rest and fascinate people with my stories. I knew damn well I would drink again. In my mind, all I had to do was stop drinking at work and stop having problems from drinking. I have to laugh at that now.

But some seeds were planted that I could use to water and grow later.

I drank a quart of beer the first day I got out of the hospital and nothing bad happened. In fact, I practiced very controlled drinking for eighteen months. I managed to keep it quite a secret and I was the only person who knew I was fucking up. Although I'm sure Fred suspected, he never stopped shaking my hand.

Fred assumed the duty of becoming my sponsor. Having been my God-parent as a child, this felt quite natural. He and Mr. Audrey, a diabetic who had lost his legs and decided to get sober at the age of 65, took me to meetings all over Northwest Ohio. I loved hearing about the crazy shit they did in their lives. I felt loved and guided for the first time. Although more than another decade was to pass before I really got sober, this time in my life was very important to me.

Fred developed cancer in his jaw in the last few years of his life. After several operations which resulted in the loss of the left side of his jaw, the doctors gave him a bleak prognosis. A once handsome and stunning man developed rapidly into a man who was painful to behold. Fred was a tough old fuck. I occasionally saw tears well up in his eyes but rarely did I see them fall.

Because of the operations Fred had a constant dribble. Many nerves in his face no longer worked nor did his sinuses or mucous membranes. At some point he got a severe cold which eventually left him hooked on Nyquil. At that time Nyquil was 25% alcohol. He collected all the newspapers he could, clipping out the coupons and leaving Rite Aid with huge bottles of the stuff. At first, no one except the people there suspected anything was going on.

One night his wife called asking me to get over there as quickly as I could. "He's out of his mind, Bill."

When I arrived Fred was stark-ass naked, walking around the house mumbling something about wanting to fuck his sister-in-law. "Fred, what the fuck are you doing?" I asked him but got no coherent response.

I called some buddies from AA over to help. We laughed our asses off when we went through the garbage and found all the Nyquil bottles. His wife knew enough about addiction by now to know this was not Fred's fault. She made coffee for us and he slept it off.

I miss Fred. I miss his big hands giving me reassurance. Though dormant for many years, he helped plant seeds and keep them fertile so that when the time was right for me, they would be fruitful. They grew the entire seven years I binged after I lost the career that originally defined my life.

And now I bear bright purple violets and velvety green leaves that bruise every now and again when you press them too hard, but glisten and glow when you mist them gently with love and hope.

MY LAST NIGHT AS A POLICE OFFICER

It was on April 3, 1983 that I worked my last shift on the police department. I'd been partying quite heavily at my brother-in-law's and normally wouldn't have gone to work in that severe of condition. However, both the Captain and Sergeant were off that night leaving me, the senior officer in charge. I thought I'd be able to get away with it. I was wrong.

Shortly after reporting for duty at midnight I noticed my buzz was already wearing off. My addiction kicked in and was making me increasingly uncomfortable. After waiting as long as tolerable, I entered 7-11 without a plan as the hands on the clock approached 2:00 a.m. My shaking became visible. I needed to get some drinks in me--fast.

"Officer," asked the trusting clerk, "could you keep an eye on things while I run to the restroom? I've been holding it and I gotta GO," she emphasized.

"Of course," I said too eagerly. Without hesitation I walked directly to the wine display area and stuffed a fifth of Wild Irish Rose down the front of my pants and zipped up my jacket to conceal the bottle. Here I am . . . a cop, in charge of the shift that night, going through withdrawal at the local convenience store, watching the counter while the clerk takes a piss . . . stealing a cheap ass bottle of wine. Any length to have a drink. Any God damn length.

Holding my breath, I put the bottle to my lips and gulped down one third of it as soon as I was seated safely in the cruiser. Heading for the south side of town, assuming if life in Fostoria remained quiet I could rejoin the party, I put the bottle back to my mouth and drank another third. Then I thought "Fuck it" and that fifth of Wild Irish Rose was gone in less than ten minutes.

Hitting the tree head on must have shaken my body up pretty hard because it woke me up. I had no idea what had occurred or how much time had passed. Reacting quickly, I grabbed the police radio and lied to the dispatcher.

"I was just run off the road by a speeding vehicle. The vehicle is now heading north from the south end of town."

Two cruisers parked a few blocks north of where I was located radioed back to inform me there was no such vehicle entering from the south. I was caught.

Because I wrecked the patrol car just outside of town in the country, the sheriff had to be called. Both the cruisers parked close came to check on me. The entire left side of my car was heavily damaged. The fender was practically wrapped around the windshield and obscured my vision. The left front tire was flat. I panicked. Everyone at the scene would now watch me drive that fucked up car back to the station and know I fucked up . . . and tried to lie about it.

Upon arriving at the station I called in all the units to inform them I was going home sick and to pass on the chain of command to the next senior officer. Protocol was to notify my shift commander of the accident. One of my fellow officers had to make that call; I just wanted to go home and pretend this didn't happen.

I burst through the front door at home and landed face first on the couch, fully uniformed, gun belt and all, before passing out. My second wife, whom I had startled out of a deep sleep, came out of the bedroom long enough for me to tell her I had really fucked up and they'd be knocking on the door before long.

"I'm letting them in," she said, completely fed up with me. I was too drunk to put up a fight.

At about four o'clock that morning, I awoke to a knock. The Captain and the Chief stood serious and somber at my door. In spite of how drunk I still felt, the events which followed were sobering.

They informed me that I was near my brother-in-law's house when I passed out and lost control of the cruiser. Apparently, a retrace of my trail revealed that I had run up into two adjacent yards, taking out both of their fences. Next I drove straight up into another yard where the street ended and struck a telephone pole. Then I proceeded to hit one tree and another, which ultimately woke me up.

They produced a piece of paper which required my signature to serve as an official resignation. The deal was that if I resigned tonight I would retain my retirement benefits and the city's insurance would pay for all the property damage. I had to agree to never again apply for any job with any department in the city of Fostoria.

"Please," I plead for just a moment, requesting more treatment for my alcoholism. "Give me one more chance- it might work this time."

"We already woke up the City Solicitor," said the Chief.

His name was on the typewritten resignation. I signed it.

That moment is a permanent part of my memory. My lifelong dream to be a cop was all fucked up forever. My friends were down here handing me the resignation I deserved. I couldn't separate my alcoholism from me, and blamed me entirely. I had shamed my entire family, my children. I decided I was truly a piece of shit. They left and I drank all the beer in the refrigerator.

It calmed me down and provided some relief. I remember feeling relieved that I had never seriously hurt someone. Relieved that I'd never been caught doing any of the things which would have sent me to prison where I'd have to spend the entire time in lock down because I'd

been a cop. I was relieved, on some level, that whatever was going to happen as a result of my

actions that night, and on many nights before, had just happened. It was over.

At approximately nine o'clock that morning, Deputy Orr was at my home requesting him

that I meet him at the police department to file the appropriate paperwork. There was no reason

to be uncooperative.

He presented me with two citations. One was for failure to stay on the paved portion of

the roadway and one was for leaving the scene of an accident. The latter was dismissed due to

the fact that I had twenty four hours to report the property damage. Only seven hours had

passed. Thank you Deputy Orr.

What follows this horrifying night, my last night as a police officer, is the beginning of a

drinking and drugging binge that is to last for seven years. Seven sad, scary, long, and lonely

years.

BLEEDING OUT

Morning always met me soaking in my own sweaty toxin-concoction of alcohol, heroin, cocaine, marijuana or whatever else I'd siphoned into me the night before. This morning began no differently. Until I sat up.

The sheets, the pillow case, the blanket, everything was bright red. Leaping from the bed in a total panic I attempted to clear the short six or seven steps to the bathroom. But I stumbled over my own lifeless limbs and bounced off the hallway wall onto the soft clean carpet. Everything went black.

"Oh my God! Oh my God! OH MY GOD! Dad . . . Dad . . . Dad . . . Dad- are you awake- Dad what's wrong- DAD! WAKE UP DAD!" The voice belonged to one of my children. She hovered over me screaming. She shook my shoulders and sat me up. "There's blood coming from your EARS! It's running out of your mouth . . . what do I do? Dad!? What should I do? Holy shit- Jesus Christ. This is so FUCKED up . . ." Her voice trailed off. I put my finger to my mouth, then my ears. She was right. I blinked a few times to make things look clearer. She was gone.

The next thing I remember is standing in front of the refrigerator opening a can of beer. My daughter told me my previous sponsor was on the way over to take me to the Emergency Room. I polished off a six pack before he arrived and took four in the car ride to the hospital. Or so I've been told. Personally, I don't remember anything between the refrigerator and the Critical Care Unit at Saint Vincent's Hospital in Toledo.

A hazy fog tunneled my vision from that hospital bed. A bag full of bloody red liquid hung to my right. It was being drained from my stomach through a tube in my nose. A fidgeting doctor came in and looked from the bag to my stomach, to the ceiling, and then straight into my eyes.

"Mr. Hammer, I would strongly encourage you to call your family, your loved ones. You know, anyone you might want to see again. He waited for a reply. I shook my head no and closed my eyes. "Think about it" he said. *"I am already dead"* I thought. I lay there like that for three days.

Emotionally, I have no idea what happened over that seventy two hour period. Sensibly, a man may use such a time for reflection and contemplation. He may think profound thoughts and ponder the meaning of existence. He may imagine his family at his funeral. See his wife kiss his cheek one final time and adjust his tie. Hear his sons say "I wish I'd played more baseball with Dad." Smell his daughter's perfume as she gently places the little locket he gave her for Christmas in the fourth grade into his palm for a peaceful passage from this life into the next one. Feel the wind blow his sprayed stiff hair. Taste the burnt coffee everyone is pretending to drink. This man did none of those things. This man lay like a carcass waiting for death to claim him and wondered why it was taking so long

I was too numb to feel anything for anyone, least of all me.

On day four I awoke with a half dozen or so white coated men standing around my bed using some big clinical language I did not understand. I looked over at the bag. The substance inside it was clean today, not even a trace of red. Each doctor spoke, offering some mumble-jumble opinion but ultimately ending with the sentence that they had no real good explanation for what happened.

"It looks like you're going to pull through. However, Mr. Hammer, it is very likely that the next drink you take could kill you. Do you understand the severity of this?" I nodded yes. And I did understand. I just didn't care.

I was released from the hospital and laid on the couch for a few days to "recover." My family wrapped me in blankets and brought me glasses of water occasionally. I slept and went to the bathroom.

As soon as I felt well enough, I had a drink.

LETTER

Dear Bill,

A depression has descended upon me the likes of which I have never experienced. As if the gloomy gray sky has fallen directly on my shoulders, I trudge through the moments, hours, days, one undistinguishable from the next, trying to hoist the empty weight of it in the hopes it drops no further. In the hopes it drops not to my chest, suffocating me. In the hopes it drops not to my hips, forcing me to birth it's pain. In the hopes it drops not to my knees, bringing me to them

Dense with fog, absent of any semblance of life, I hear Drew Carey say "And this showcase can be yours, if The Price is Right." His is the only voice in our home.

I can see you, sitting silently in your chair. A cup of coffee, filmed with a layer of cream cools on the table to your right. Your eyelids shutter, fighting sleep. I wonder if you know you are dying. I wonder if I should have told you?

I watched you wither, like a parched October leaf, crinkling and aimless, blowing through a yard where an oblivious child plays. A childe unaware that there are indefinable pains heavier than the weight of the new bicycle Dad puts on the porch for safe keeping each night.

"I need to get my strength back. Why am I so tired? I just can't wake up. Maybe I'll feel better tomorrow" you assert before sliding on your slippers and resigning yourself to bed. The Family Feud has just started. One out of one hundred people surveyed, all of them will miss you. Particularly me.

I miss you.

Love, your adoring wife- Jenn

LETTER

Dear Bill,

Like an icy snowball being pushed uphill, my life collects all the debris in its path. The snowball, once manageable in the palm of my hand, twinkling and glistening with white and purity, is now brown-splotched and monstrous. It is out of my control; it is so much bigger than me. Twigs poke out as if trying to scratch me while I gasp for air, clench my muscles, and shove behind it. My thighs scream at me to collapse, let it roll back down, smack into a tree and break into thousands of pieces like shards of glass from a fragile vase.

But I keep on pushing. I don't know why. Do I think I have to beat the snowball? Do I think something glorious will happen once I get it to the top? Do I think letting it go would be a reflection of my inability to do what must be done?

I saw you last night in my dreams. It was so great to touch you. Being your wife was one of the greatest joys of my life. I remember drinking hot chocolate with you while you taught me how to play backgammon. Your sturdy, gently hands methodically lining up the pieces of the game, the way you touched everything in your life . . . with care, good intentions. It is the way I need to touch that snowball now. Pull the twigs out, learn to love the smears that have clung to it, nudge it along the best I can until it's atop the hill and can stand on its own.

I miss you.

Love, your adoring wife- Jenn

PATERNAL GRANDPARENTS

My grandpa Joe drank daily as long as I knew him; he was quite a phenomena. In the last few years of his life he drank 12 beers each day, strategically patterned in four hour intervals. At ten o'clock in the morning he drank four beers. At two o'clock in the afternoon he drank four beers. At six o'clock in the evening he drank four beers. Years before, Grandpa had gotten a DUI and was extremely displeased with my father who could not "just take care of it" as he served briefly as a police officer. Apparently, his solution was simply to exercise more control over his drinking.

A retired farmer who had also done some security work at Atlas Crankshaft, my grandfather was a very important man in my life. I lived with my paternal grandparents the year I went to kindergarten for the second time. Before taking me to Bryant school in the mornings he cooked me breakfast. Grandpa Joe was a kind giant who weighed well over 200 pounds and probably stood at least 6'2". So breakfast was typically bacon, eggs, ham, and home fries. He had long since taken over kitchen duties as my grandmother had developed debilitating rheumatoid arthritis and hadn't walked since my father was in his late teens. From her chair in the kitchen she instructed the family how to cook, sew, can foods, and all the jobs she had done prior. We always had plenty of canned corn, beets, jams, jellies, and beans. When I became an EMT, I once took Grandma out of the house for the first time in decades using the ambulance. Her knees had calcified and hurt so badly by then she was unable to even bend them. She was such a bit of a thing. I carefully lifted her out of the bed and placed her gently on the gurney. Her eyes grew large from the back of the ambulance as we drove around and opened the doors at various places so she could see the changes which had taken place. Despite all her pain, I never once heard her complain. What a kind woman. On occasion she would tell me to grab the phone book she kept on the stand beside her bed. When their money came in, she told my grandpa

which bills needed paid and the remainder was given to her for safe keeping. Strategically

placed throughout the pages was all their money in cash; ones here, fives there, tens back here.

"Turn to about the middle, honey, and take a dollar for yourself. Go buy yourself some

candy." She never told me to save it or any of those things kids hate doing with the money

they've been given.

One morning I sat beside her bed while she ate breakfast; bread with butter and coffee

every morning. The front door opened right into her bedroom, which would have functioned as

the living room in most people's homes. "Go out there into the bureau and get into my box," she

whispered, smiling. "Go ahead, get yourself a piece of candy." She had an incredible sense of

hearing and smell as well. She called for my grandpa as he came up the basement stairs.

"Has he been down there with you this morning?" I heard her ask. And I had. Against

one wall of the basement was lined a row of 55 gallon drums filled with my grandfather's

delicious homemade wine from his own vineyard. Occasionally he'd let me dink half a glass or

so and I got a little giggly. She had smelled it on me and berated him quite thoroughly. "Joe!

What are you doing? He's only a little boy!" I never heard her swear once.

After that we went out to Grandpa's five acres of land on which he grew a garden with

every imaginable vegetable. He kept it on a separate piece of property which he called his farm.

He lifted me up with his huge hands, which were soft and kind despite being slightly deformed

from years of hard work. He sat me down on the seat of his tractor and helped me start it up.

Grandpa bent down and let me pat his bald head. "You're the only one I let do that," he said.

Grandpa Joe took me to Son's Bar and Grill with him a few times though I was instructed

never to tell. "Just say we went out to my farm," he'd wink at me. We didn't stay long. He drank a couple shots of whisky with a short glass of beer as a chaser without having to order. Grandma never knew that he was considered a regular there. Most of our conversations there were about my dad. "He was strong as a bull," Grandpa would say, after a drink or two. A natural athlete, my father was an extremely talented pitcher. He had tried out for the Cleveland Indians and had made the team shortly after high school. Within weeks of his good news he came home one night to find my grandfather sitting at the table holding a piece of paper. It was his notice to report for service; it was World War II. Obviously, his opportunity to play baseball was ruined and never presented itself again. Grandpa said my father was never again quite the same.

I don't know if my grandfather knew he was an alcoholic. I don't know if he thought life dealt him an unfair hand. I don't know if he watched other couples grow old together--sitting on their front porches drinking iced tea on warm summer evenings, taking walks in the fluffy white snow on Christmas Eve, carrying picnic baskets into the park as the flowers came up in early spring--and thought *why me?* I do know I watched him steadily deteriorate after my grandmother died. I do know he looked lonely after she wasn't in her bedroom any more. And I do know he died several years later of a broken heart.

LETTER

Dear Bill,

Nine years ago today, on September 15, 2001 you moved to Findlay to be with me, leaving Fostoria forever. How the sun shone brightly that Saturday nearing autumn. How my heart leapt inside my chest!

Hundreds of Saturdays have passed since then. Saturdays served up to us like bagels and lox to royalty. Saturdays taken off our laps like neatly folded napkins. Spring Saturdays spent walking hand in hand at Riverbend Park, allowing the green of the new leaves to ease our pain at that which is temporary, watching the tadpoles turn into frogs. Summer Saturdays, spent lounging in the pool, listening to Nina Simone remind you "I put a spell on you", smelling the fat drip as you grilled your famous steaks. Fall Saturdays spent sleeping in until you gently ran your finger down my arm, kissed my cheek, and woke me with fresh coffee and French toast in bed. Winter Saturdays spent huddled under the covers, intertwined so closely we became one, making love until darkness blanketed us again and you said, laughing "We better get some food in us!"

I recall a Saturday this last February. It was six days after what I knew would be our last Valentine's Day together. I hadn't the heart to tell you yet. Your head then bald, your eyes sunken in from exhaustion, your body starting to wither from the toll of chemo. Another man would have found a way to stay home that day. Another man would have said "Not today. It's too cold." But not you. Not this man. You put on a hat, a sweatshirt, a coat, a couple pairs of socks and you took my car to get the oil changed.

"I'm so grateful" you said, after hanging my keys up when you returned "that my being responsible for myself does not mean I'm out in search of a drink. I'm so grateful for other reasons too. Some say addicts and alcoholics are on a path to a slow suicide. I'll tell you, that's a lonely way to die." As I sit here typing now I realize you wondered, too. Would this be your

last winter? Our last Valentine's Day? Another man would have felt sorry for himself. He may

have screamed at God. He may have yelled "Why me? Why now? What have I done to deserve

this?" You were just grateful you were dying sober and not alone. You were just grateful to

have a chance to fight for your life. And fight, you did.

I miss you Bill. I miss your green van. I miss that one bedroom apartment we started out

in on Hardin Street. I miss that horrible pink bathtub and that ridiculous linoleum on the

bathroom floor. I miss walking down that long hall with you on that wretched brown carpet,

smelling a dozen other tenants' dinners' wafting out under the cracks of their doors.

I miss you.

Love, Your adoring wife- Jenn

ON BEING TOUCHED

This is going to sound crazier than fuck.

My father never did come back for us in Detroit so I guess we went looking for him.

Half way through my first year in kindergarten my mother told me one winter day that we were

moving to Fostoria, Ohio. I didn't have to go to school right away when we moved because

something about having to be five years old to start school in this state. That was okay with me.

I missed Nana but loved my paternal grandparents, too. We stayed with them until the summer I

was six and had just repeated kindergarten.

We lived in the bottom half of a modest duplex. In the biggest front yard I'd ever seen I

had erected my very own homemade tent. With the aid of some clothesline and some

clothespins, I draped several old blankets into various positions creating a safe little haven for

which only I knew the secret entrance.

My favorite items were stored in my tent: coloring books, crayons, lead army men my

father made for me with some kit, and my cowboy outfit. While I personally preferred to be the

Indian, my parents had bought me a dark blue cowboy hat; a short, fringed, white vest; little

brown chaps; and black toy pistols that hung on either side in my little kid hip-holsters. I was

hysterical. In my fantasy land, this yard was a vast and mysterious forest full of adventure and

intrigue. One moment I could be found lurking in the tall, swampy grasses of Africa, hunting

antelope for food and hiding from the lion, king of the jungle. The next moment I was the

sheriff, galloping on my horse through a once law abiding town now corrupt by a mustached

train robber who tied a damsel to the tracks to distract me. But his ruse was not cunning enough

as I both arrested the robber and rescued the damsel. Actually, I never have been able to hunt in

my adult life and continue to fish without a hook on my line. As for arresting the robbers and rescuing the damsels, the fine line between good guy and bad guy got blurry during my cop

years, and the distressed damsel I thought I rescued once slipped some angel dust into my joint

and attempted to perform an exorcism on me. That is a different story.

My mother was kind to me that summer. In her flowery housecoats she called me in

before bed time and I got to eat a peanut butter and grape jelly sandwich and drink a glass of

milk. I loved them. They meant more to me at that time than I could have realized. My mother

was not always kind to me. There were no hugs; there were no kissed skinned knees. There

were no "I love you's" or stories before nap times. There was no one to tell me to brush my teeth

after I ate or wash my hands before dinner. For this and many reasons, that summer stands out.

I had never before experienced the connection between touch and love.

The first time I remember being touched in a meaningful way was by a neighbor girl

named Roberta, who was four or five years older than me. She visited my side of the street

infrequently. On one occasion she came into my yard wanting to know what I kept in my tent.

Playing a pirate that day, I feared she had anchored her ship on the other side of the deserted

island where she hid a band of thieves who wanted my treasures. After I questioned her

thoroughly, she was bid welcome into my secret entrance. But once inside, Roberta did

something she had never done before. She fondled me.

I did not know how to respond so I let her touch me. It felt good. Confusing, but good.

It was a feeling that I never had. How crazy I've felt for so many years about my mixed

emotions regarding this five minute period of my life where I first experienced the feeling that I

was worth being touched and that being touched gently, felt good.

FLAWS

Findlay, Ohio was extra humid the August Bill died. Sitting in the garage on our green lawn chairs, sweat dripping from my forehead, I watched the parade of friends and family who came to say goodbye to my husband. There were no floats or bands. Just lost faces and mouths moving, dropping words from lips that didn't really know what to say.

Both of his sisters and both of his brothers visited. He had turned out to be a good big brother. They hoped he got to see their dad . . . I hope he told them he was grateful they came but I don't know if he had the strength.

Visibly shaken and frequently needing breaks outside, his mom made her way to the patio, sat down on the swing, dropped her cane, and cried silently, not wanting to be consoled. Though I never asked, I wondered about the 63 years of tape rewinding and fast forwarding in her head. Theirs was a vase never super glued, but not thrown away either. "I am proud of you" she told him. "I always have been."

From the baby monitor in the garage, Fuji, Karen, and I listened while Josh, our longtime family friend, gave Bill all the basketball updates. "Shaq went to The Celtics. Z went to Miami with LeBron . . ."

Jodi and Raye kissed him on the forehead and fought tears. "We love you Billy Butt" they told him. Having lost his father to pancreatic cancer a few years prior, Tim was unable to come in the room; it was just too much to bear.

Jim and Karen promised to take care of his granddaughters. Fuji and I promised to take care of each other.

Unburdening the heart to the dying is no easy task. Unburdening the heart of the dying is like trying to convince a sleepy and temperamental child he doesn't need a new transformer today when his birthday is tomorrow.

While my husband could no longer talk, I knew the burdens of his heart. Some of us thought he continued to cling to life long after his body stopped working in an effort to make it to our anniversary. Others thought he was afraid to meet his maker, having struggled his entire life with forgiving the sins of his youth, his addictive behavior, his general mistakes. Bill forgave the most heinous acts of others, sins I could have never overlooked... but seemed unable to extend that forgiveness to himself. He had not spoken in three days. I would not make the mistake I had made years before. I made the call and Father Mike administered Last Rites, the anointing of the sick, the day Bill finally left his body forever. Standing silently in the kitchen, I listened in the other baby monitor as Father Mike told him it was time to go home and be with God. I did not cry; in fact I felt little other than relief for Bill. They were words he needed to hear.

I suppose all funerals are alike and dissimilar. Someone has died. We honor their life, busy ourselves with the tasks of choosing caskets, flowers, writing eulogies. How we knew and we loved the deceased is our own unique experience.

Bill had watched so many people die. One morning in the late 1980's he awoke, as he often had during that time, in a local flop house. Stale beer, vomit, rotting wounds... the usual stench filled his nostrils. He slithered from bottle to bottle, searching for his first drink. Zach, whose parents died when he was little, slept next to Bill on the couch. A Wild Irish Rose drinker, Zach had lived his entire life with a deformity on his right foot that made walking difficult. One morning, years later, he was found in someone's front yard, having died of an aneurysm in his stomach that killed him as he bled to death after a night of drinking.

On a makeshift bed of pillows and cushions, slept Bertha that morning. An infrequent visitor to the Flophouse, she was one of the guys, and a sharer. Bertha solicited funds on

occasion to purchase a bottle of liquor, her preference, and everyone got a drink. Having never

enjoyed her life, alcoholism took it from her before she ever reached fifty.

A needled dangled from the injection site on Scott's arm. He was passed out face down

on the kitchen table that particular day. Athletically built, Scott was a strong, angry man who

never felt calm until the day he began injecting Heroin. Several years later he was found dead in

an apartment on the East side of Detroit. He had overdosed.

I don't know where Bill went when his body quit working. His ashes are in a travel urn I

take with me nearly every place I go. I am not opposed to a place called Heaven, though I don't

really know where it would be. If my husband is there, I hope he has enjoyed a good game of

Texas Hold 'Em with Zach, Bertha, and Scott.

I hope he and Jerry are on a warm, breezy cruise along with all the other American and

Vietnamese soldiers who died during that war.

I hope he has gone to the races and had ice cream with his dad.

I hope he and his grandparents have been out in the garden, ridden on the tractor, had

bread and coffee for breakfast.

I hope he plays catch with those little boys who died in that fire.

I hope he and his first wife dance.

Bill's funeral was on a Saturday, 2 days before what would have been our seventh

anniversary. A sunny, windless day, it was the kind you would anticipate following a long

unexpected storm. Around two hundred people came to pay their respects. Client after client

approached me to share what Bill had meant to them in his years as their counselor.

Having neglected myself in the process of taking care of my husband, my roots were showing dark while the bulk of my head was blonde from the summer sun and chlorine. The humidity made an afro of my naturally curly hair. I'd forgotten to buy any hose and I'd run out of lipstick. I'd gained sixty pounds. And in my black and white dress I looked perfect. Bill taught me that. I didn't know how perfectly flawed I was until he loved me.

On our anniversary I received a colorful, gorgeous bouquet of flowers signed simply "Love, BSM." Everyone who had come to know Bill through me during the course of his battle with cancer had followed my lead by shortening one of my pet names for him: Big Strong Man. If I had buried him, I would have put it on his headstone. But he specifically requested to be cremated and remain with me forever. I don't know who sent them, but I'd like to think it was him. When it's my time to leave my body, I hope he keeps his promise to come back and get me. I'll look forward to seeing him.

Bill wore an Orthocerus Stone around his neck I had given him when we first fell in love for the remainder of his life. It hangs around my neck now and beside it clanks his wedding ring. If you see me, you will find them, worn and rubbed above my heart. Sometimes on our journey, we are blessed enough to find those people, who, like The Grand Canyon on the continent, carve out such a place for themselves in our landscape, we wouldn't know ourselves without them.

They are fossils in our souls.

THE SHOE STORY

My mother loves to tell this story about me as a child.

In fact, she has told it so many times to aunts, uncles, second cousins, in-laws, neighbors, her hairdresser, her dentist, the guy in line behind her at Montgomery Ward, Mrs. Arbeson in the pew in front of us on Sundays . . . that it has almost become part of my own childhood memories.

She describes a trip home from Detroit in which, while driving steadily along I-75, I threw a brand new "walking shoe" out the window. She continually chooses to tell this story as though a two-year-old were consciously capable of throwing a shoe out the window with any purpose whatsoever. In all the times I've heard this story, lively with its "Can you imagine?", finger tips tapping above her heart, rolling eyes and raising brows, I've never heard her use words like "innocent" or "precious." Rather, she enjoys using words like "mischievous" and "ungrateful."

"Jesus Christ, you know we had to go back and try to find it," she shrugs her shoulders slightly forward and turns her forearms up with clenched fists. "And in all that traffic. We never found the God damned thing." My mother's swearing was always a source of embarrassment for me. Here I was, learning about the torturous hell in which one may be eternally banned for sins such as taking the Lords name in vain, and my reformed Catholic mother let those words roll loosely and regularly off her sharp tongue.

Although my mother has witnessed my reddening face, squirming posture, and curled upper lip, she chooses to belittle me by telling this story--repeatedly. There will always be an again. She enjoys this brief, yet petty method of punishment. An opportunist, my mother uses this story to remind me that I was a chore to her, a lesson in labor. Never a gift or a joy, never a little boy to watch giggle and play.

Sometimes I wish she would forgo the drama. She could just say "Bill- well he was this kid who was never doing things right."

Sometimes I wish she would tell the story about how I won the City Marble Championship in 1958. That summer I participated in a city wide recreation program where I got to make wallets and pottery, play softball and checkers, and feel like I was good at something.

But the highlight of the summer was the final match between myself and Cecil Wilmington as we crouched on the playground black top, exposed knees and all, with 50 kids circling us and yelling "C'mon Bill" and "C'mon Cecil!"

That morning I polished my favorite shooter, a fiery red puree. I never actually expected to win. I assumed Cecil was better than me. I assumed everyone was better than me. But Cecil would go on teach me about winning, losing, and friendship. Although he attended Fostoria high school and I, Saint Wendelin, he often picked me for his team at Sunday afternoon scrimmages. During the holidays we worked together at "Mitches Men and Boys Wear" for extra cash. It was at his wedding reception, years later, that I would get really drunk, and in front of my first wife, kick the shit out of the man who was married to the woman I secretly loved. Although provoked, I was drinking heavily and, consequently, making stupid decisions. Alcohol completely erased my interest in how others felt. Always polite, Cecil had responded by saying, after I had virtually destroyed the happiest day of his life, "Bill, I didn't expect this out of you."

My eye was on that day and despite hitting nothing on my first turn I knocked four marbles out of the circle on my second turn. Cecil knocked out two and then failed to connect on the third shot of his second turn. I won, knocking out my sixth marble on the second shot of my third turn. Cecil was gracious and I was delighted. All the neighborhood kids cheered for me as we were at Whittier school on my home turf. Mr. Boroff, the organizer of the event, awarded me a tee-shirt reading "City Marble Championship 1958." I was so proud. This is my happiest childhood memory. It was the most worry free time of my entire life.

I narrated the day's events to my family at the dinner table that night, mimicking the flick of my finger into the marble and the sound of the kids in the crowd. I laid my shirt over my chest and held it up with my chin while I ran my hands across the lettering.

My dad ate mashed potatoes and my mother wiped her hand on the baby's bib.

I have never heard her tell this story.

NINE DAYS

It took Bill nine days to die. Fuji had been with us for six weeks, since he decided to stop

chemo. He nodded yes when I asked "Honey, do you understand what is happening?" But he

didn't. Moments later he would ask "How long has Karen been here?" Bill's daughter-in-law

moved right in with Fuji and me to see him through to the end. They were both helping keep a

promise I'd made to Bill on November 19, 2010. The oncologist had given us the news we

dreaded that day. He had Small Cell Lung Cancer and it was terminal. He was going to do die.

There was little I could do for my husband at that moment except reassure him I would be with

him every step of the journey and promise him he would die in his own bed, on his own pillow,

in his own room, in his own home.

He pounded his weakened, balled up fists on his hospital bed. "I don't want to die. I just

want more time- with you." Bill was not afraid to cry in front of me. But even I had never seen

him like this.

Bill had once spent nine days saving his own life. Weighing only 128 pounds in the

summer of 1990, he decided it was finally time to stop drinking. Accustomed to anywhere up to

30 drinks a day, and having suffered alcohol withdrawal related seizures previously, he was

terrified. I guess he decided he was more afraid of dying in his condition at the time. "The

sound of the shower" during those years scared him he once confessed. He knew the water

would hurt his skin. Rarely bathing as a result, Bill spent the bulk of his days drinking, eating a

cheeseburger here or there at a bar every few days, and trying to avoid mirrors.

He wasn't going to the hospital this time, either, he decided. Instead, Bill would titrate

and attempt to detox himself at home.

Slowly, hoping to minimize the withdrawal symptoms as much as possible, he drank 12 beers on his first day. He described his chest pounding, as if an elephant sat on top. "What if I have a seizure at home?" he though, "I could die." Dry heaving and gut wrenching, he pressed on. The second day he drank 12 beers as well. Often, he was scarcely able to hold the can as his body shook violently from the inside out. He managed to cover all the windows with heavy dark blankets and shut out the world.

He drank 10 beers on the third day. "Every cell in me screamed for more," he shared. Frequently finding himself curled up in a ball on the floor with no recollection of how he got there, Bill thought, *I am going to die. Maybe tonight. Maybe in the morning. But I am going to die. I have taken this too far.* A weakness overcame him on day four. Like a carpet saturated with cleaning solution and never swept up, a heavy, melancholic hopelessness overcame him. He drank 8 beers.

There was really nothing left in him to throw up but alcohol and on the fifth day he drank 8 more beers. Not yet even convinced he would survive, he knew it had been a while since he had last eaten, but could not recall for sure. He stopped wrenching on the sixth day and consumed 6 beers. It was enough to ward off a seizure, but that was about all.

Bill drank 4 beers on the seventh day and 2 beers on the eighth. Unable to remember much of those last two days, he knew only that at some point on the 4th of July he left his house for the first time since attempting to go through withdrawal at home in an effort to attend the fireworks display. Looking disastrous, he was physically incapable of showering, shaving, brushing his teeth, or tending to his hygiene in any way. He was too weak to even get out of the car.

He had done it though. July 6, 1990 arrived and Bill did not have a drink. In fact, he never drank again. Twenty years passed. Twenty years. Recovery. Healing. Helping.

Amends. Acceptance. Trying. Hoping.

Twenty years had passed when he stood in front of me on Friday July 2, 2010. The

morning sunlight poured in through the front bay window and cast a glow around his

deteriorated frame. Begging for me to understand, his eyes found mine. "I don't think I have

much time left honey. I am sorry" he said quietly and matter-of-factly.

"It's okay cutie. One person only has the right to expect so much from another." I

hugged him. Bill and I had always seen one another in the way each of us had spent our lives

trying to be seen. It was good enough. It would have to be.

He didn't have any more chemo after that. There were no more doctor appointments, no

more accessing his port, no more x-rays or MRIs. Just the Hospice nurses now. And morphine,

phenargran, ativan, haldol, pill crushing . . .

During that time, Bill ate his last gyro from Charlie's, licked his last vanilla ice cream

cone from Archie's, walked for the last time barefoot on the grass at our home on Cynthia Court,

heard where LeBron James would play his next season for the last time, read his last hometown

newspaper, "The Courier," and took his last ride by Riverside Park.

We tried to get as much of his last wishes in as his defeated body and mind would

tolerate.

Nine days before he died, whatever little bit of life remained in my husband appeared to

evaporate like a fog over a lake burnt off by the dawn. It was Tuesday, August 17, 2010. "I will

fight until the day I wake up and there's no fight left in me." I guess that was the day. He spent

much of that time in his bed. As if it had been pumped into the house through the central air

conditioning, we all knew it, too. Everything those nine days got too clear, too vivid, too

succinct, too crisp. Like the English language had adopted a K in every word. Smack. Hark.

Fuck. Rock. Chunk. Wake. Kick. Rake. It all felt like that.

We did everything possible to keep those K's out of his room, too. He'd had enough of them.

"Am I going to die soon?" he asked. "Yes, honey, you are," I told him. "When?" he inquired. "Well, a lot of that depends on you," I took his hand. "How do you mean?" Bill looked desperate for the answer. "When you're ready," I smiled, hoping to restore some sense of control for him. "I'm ready, this has gotten too hard," he replied. And it really had.

My husband could not move or speak for the final three days of his life. Occasionally, he was able to squeeze a hand to indicate we had gotten him in a comfortable position. Sometimes, when he heard my voice enter the room he attempted to follow me with his eyes. Karen, Fuji, and I sang to him, which sometimes made him smile. He seemed to favor "Amazing Grace" and "I'm a Little Tea Pot."

When Bill came home from the ICU the prior fall, after he'd gotten terribly sick following his liver Biopsy, I'd sent everyone on our friends, colleagues, and family email list a message. I told them my husband needed hope more than he needed anything and we would be focusing on living rather than dying. I said my final words to my husband would be "See you tomorrow" in this spirit. I had forgotten about this during those nine days.

At 10:34 p.m. on Thursday August 26, 2010 I kissed my husband, told him good night and said "See you tomorrow cutie." He took his last breath at 10:37. And then his soul left his body. I told him I was very proud of him and shut his eyes.

We gave him a bath, washed and trimmed his hair, shaved his face, brushed his teeth, cleaned up his eyebrows, and put on dry fresh clothes for him. Bill was not leaving his home for the last time looking the way he did that 4th of July in 1990. Not as my husband. Not the most handsome man I'd ever seen.

I crawled into bed and held him as long as I could until the men from the funeral home came for his body.

I could not watch them take him from the house knowing he was never coming back. I heard the doors shut in the driveway and the car pull out. I knew he was in the back, lying calmly and without pain for the first time in a long time. The light flickered off and on in his room until 4:00 that morning as Fuji and Karen cleaned up his sheets and bed. It never happened before and has not happened since.

LETTER

Dear Bill,

It's about two weeks before Christmas. I've made it through what would have been your 64th birthday and the anniversary of the day we met twelve years ago. I tried to write you both times but had to stop.

Watching you suffer all those months has left me a bit raw. Sometimes thinking about it makes my stomach sick. I've felt small and powerless before. I suppose we all have. When you visit in my dreams, the one's where you know you are dying, I want to give you more than I have to give. But I wake up and you are still gone. I could not save you, even in my sleep.

Being alone is not as hard as I thought it would be at times. I sleep when I want, go where I want, watch what I want, and do what I want. I supposed I've found some freedom in finality. I just wanted you to know it's not all bad.

I laugh at some point almost every day now. I remember the funny things you said towards the end. Like when you said "I'm going to run away from this place" and I told you could as soon as you took your medicine. And when, in a rapid startled voice you informed me "Fuji saw my pee-pee" after she had taken you to the bathroom.

Spending the holidays alone in our house seemed a bit much so I've come to CT to celebrate them with Fuji's family. Yesterday we baked Christmas cookies and we've even put up a tiny Christmas tree. I'm sure you are aware I sing carols at the top of my lungs and annoy all in hearing range.

It hasn't snowed yet but when it does I will remember the Christmas Eve the year I was ten. How, in the still darkness the man on Elm Street stood peacefully on his porch playing "Silent Night" on his flute. How, alone on the sidewalk, bundled in my green winter coat, I listened to every note and sung every word in my head. How the red and white Christmas lights danced quietly around the two of us, and the streetlights provided the only view of the snowy crystals falling to their new home on the ground.

And I will remember you. I will remember the peace you brought to my life. How you left it here, a treasure for me to open when I need and enjoy forever. How you knew exactly what to take and what to give.

Thank you Bill.

Love, your adoring wife- Jenn

LETTER

Dear Bill,

I have survived my first Christmas without you. The snow is piled high, like white cotton candy has been blown on the Earth in an effort to make it sweeter. You died four months ago yesterday. I said a prayer for you at Christmas dinner and asked God to tell you hi, let you know you are loved and missed.

Our first Christmas together seems so long ago now. We pulled into the safety of the car wash in Tiffin to make out and Ella Fitzgerald crooned "What are you doing New Year, New Years Eve?" on the radio.

Did I tell you often enough how much I appreciate everything you did to take care of me? How much it meant to me that you took out the trash, cleaned the pool, went grocery shopping, shoveled the sidewalks and drive way, got coffee ready for the next morning, trimmed the bushes, washed the cars, changed the sheets, put the dishes away, changed the light bulbs, cleaned the fire place, ran errands, fixed things up around the house, ran me baths, rubbed my head and legs.....

I can't imagine having had a better husband. I would do it all over again for the opportunity to say these things to you in person once more. You would smile and say "I know baby, I know."

The last three texts you sent me have been deleted from my phone. I cannot look at them anymore. I did not die. You did. You have earned the right to go in peace, without worry for how I will move on. And I have earned the right to move on. It is a slow and painful process, but I can do it. I am doing it.

Loving you, marrying you, and taking care of you have been amazing privileges in my life. You taught me so much about how to take care of myself, protect myself better, and be my own best friend. I am eternally grateful for every second we had together. They all meant something.

It is with the courage you gave me that I will live out this day, and all my days to follow.

Thank you Bill.

Love, your adoring wife- Jenn

LETTER

Dear Bill,

2011 has arrived! I sense an unfolding in the year to come, a tidy-boxed red and white checkered picnic blanket spread on the lawn before me as if preparing a comfortable location from which to enjoy the revealing.

Last night I dreamt we lived in a small basement apartment, perhaps on West Sandusky, with tiny, packed rooms separated by long halls. Food, napkins, plates, drinks, warm, soft glowing lights were everywhere. All reminders of something good to come. Your book, our book, my book, typed fresh and neat could be pulled from an aged, tan leather satchel for reading. No one we knew came. Yet, you continued to arrive with people. After making the trip on foot down to East Lincoln Street, you returned every few minutes with a hungry hobo you had found at those rail road tracks and you fed them. Does anyone even use that word anymore-- hobo?

I blinked, Bill. I blinked and years have passed. Even my relationship with words has become, at times, disagreeable. I could wake up anywhere. Nowhere. Trying to explain it to anyone but you would sound like nonsense. Gibberish.

Being human is so painful sometimes. Perhaps this is what separates us from all other species on this planet... the lengths we go to, the extremes, to cling to our dead. I want shave my head and have "Bill's wife" tattooed there in purple. I want to keep you somewhere.

"My people," you used to call them. Addicts, alcoholics, the lost, the suffering. I understand that best today.

I missed your steaks fresh from the grill on New Year's Eve, but I am okay.

If there had been one ripple in the fate of my days that could have kept me from you, I thank the Universe I do not know what that is.

Seeing humans through your eyes has made me a better person.

Thank you Bill.

Love, your adoring wife- Jenn

LETTER

Dear Bill,

I dreamt about you all night. You were everywhere around me. I'm so angry that you're never coming home. I'm so angry that my life with you is over. I'm so angry that I may be on this planet thirty, forty, fifty more years without being able to talk to you, see you, smell you, hear you.

The color is running out of the things around me. The textures are gone. Soft isn't soft anymore; it's just a place I put my hand looking for comfort, only to find a disappointing reminder that there are things under me, pulling me to them and away from you. Yellow is a muddy sign that reads "You have to stay here, we only let him go."

I can't bring you back.

And I can't follow you either.

Your death has driven a wedge between us that I can't find a way around.
And my life has done the same.

There is an invisible retractable tether that binds me to you, Bill. I'm so afraid it will break. I do not know its limits.

For now, I will be grateful that you, like the magnetic forces marrying the tide to the moon, come and go in my sleep, reminding me to allow for the ebb and flow of the waves that both crash and calm.

That is the way of the ocean.

Thank you Bill.

Love, your adoring wife- Jenn

LETTER

Dear Bill,

Why does time have to be so separated by all these days? Why can't I just wake up, find

that years have flown by and the sting of missing you but a memory tucked neatly away like

other mostly forgotten, yet retrievable thoughts?

Maybe I could start over. Go off the grid. Become a crime fighting super hero donning a

purple cape and mask. Slide in and out of people's lives almost unnoticed. Return lost white

and gray kittens, beat pedophiles to bloody pulps, explore all that is dark and light in me, eat rib

eye steaks for breakfast, forget who I was. Who we were.

My heart could pound a thousand times in my chest. My blood could race through my

veins with intention.

The limbo of my breath could be exhaled. Liberated to find its way like invisible smoke

rising from a candle… dancing, writing an unspoken language in the air… and descending upon

the carpet where it can never again be inhaled.

I could come back to life.

"I promise." Relief filled your eyes like tears every time I said this to you. You died in

your home with me at your side. You were cremated. You travel with me. You have been to

Boston, Lake Michigan, the Mystic Aquarium and the years will take us all the other places you

never got to go. I have but one promise to keep dear husband.

I have to finish this book.

The snow has scarcely stopped falling this February. This is the sixth month of my life

without you. Sunday morning, August 22 was the last time I heard you call out for me. There was no snow then. Just the morning sunlight pouring through the front door window as you sat in your wheelchair. While you were barely speaking, you had pointed from the edge of your bed to your chair, insisting Fuji take you for a stroll around the house. From the kitchen, shelled out and scared with the knowledge I was losing you, I washed the white coffee cups. Then I heard you. "Jenn! Jennifer!" you screamed. Dripping, I ran to you, knelt on the creamy carpet at the side of your chair. Your beautiful blue eyes, far away and half a world gone, met mine. "I'm here honey. I never leave the property. I promise. I'll be here." You didn't nod or respond. You simply turned your head slowly back to gaze at the recently trimmed green grass in our front yard. It was the last time you said my name.

I have to go now Bill. I can't miss you like this forever. I simply won't make it. Without sounding terribly cliché I don't know how to tell you how much I love you. How much I miss you. How grateful I am that you were once mine.

Thank you for putting your hands around my waist at the river. Thank you for meeting me at Lowe's. Thank you for showing me the bird nest out your window. Thank you for the pork loin sandwich. Thank you for the acronym only notes. Thank you for the long breaks. Thank you for swerving to miss that black dog. Thank you for everything Bill. Including, showing me how to let you go.

I will always adore you William Arthur Hammer.

My eternal gratitude and love- your widow, Jenn

"MY GRANDDAUGHTER WAS KILLED BY A DRUNK DRIVER"

It was a Saturday morning as I prepared to walk to the Big Book meeting at Dry Haven.

Ten years later I would chair that same meeting on some regular basis. I'd only been sober a few

months at this time and was attending meetings daily. I still wasn't working. My third wife gave

me a dollar here, a dollar there to put in the basket. This was all she allowed me to carry.

On this particular morning she was running a bit late for work and hadn't been to the bank

for the week. She pulled a ten dollar bill out of her purse; it was all she had. Looking at me with

squinty eyes as if to say "Should I or shouldn't I?" she slowly extended her arm and put the ten in

my hand without speaking. The expression on her face gave way to compassion and some

sorrow, too. It made me sad to wonder if she were ashamed of me.

My father often looked like he was ashamed of me. Frequently he said, quite formidably,

"You make me sick. You embarrass me. I don't want to be seen with you. Why don't you do

something about that?" Like it's my fault my complexion is broken out badly. Other than a few

"pizza face" comments at school, I don't recall much picking by my peers. But it was enough

knowing my own father was ashamed to be seen with me . . . ashamed of me.

On a rare occasion my mother had defended me during an argument between them about

my acne. "He'll out grow it for Christ's sake," her words fell like melting snow on deaf ears.

They took me to see Dr. Darnett, a dermatologist in Findlay who applied some solution to

my face which hurt like hell and made me wrench. After the stinging subsided the substance

hardened and was buffed off with a device resembling a sander. For several days following the

procedure I had to apply a topical ointment which left my skin coarse and bleeding. My mother

looked as me wordless as if to say "I'm sorry we have to do this." It was much the same look my

third wife gave me that morning as she handed me the ten dollar bill.

My eyes met hers with gratitude. It had been a long time since anyone had trusted me with anything. There was certainly no one to blame for that- not even me. Addiction had taken me places I do not ever remember choosing to go.

Earlier that year I'd sold a 1974 Olds Delta Royale, worth about $1500, for $400 to pay some of the bills I'd neglected. Heroin and alcohol stole precedence. There was one car left in the family-- a Mercury Bobcat I'd wrecked several times. Both doors had been replaced twice and were primered different colors of gray. I prided myself on making all repairs on the same day of the accident. In my sick mind, this prevented me from feeling too guilty and didn't allow for the expression of anger on the part of anyone else. My wife drove the Bobcat to work. I left for my three block walk to the meeting in the big white brick building where everyone would blow smoke, gulp coffee, shake my hand, and say "Glad you're here."

I started feeling too good as I stepped off the grass of my yard and onto the black top of the funeral home parking lot next door. The breeze smelled invigorating on this pleasant day in early fall and I had ten dollars in my pocket for the first time in almost three months. Suddenly the thought came over me, "I could skip that meeting altogether and head over to Doug's Tavern and get me some double shots. Hell, I could get shit faced and still be recovered by the time she comes home."

I fought that thought. I said the serenity prayer repeatedly. "I CAN NOT do this just one time" I tried to remind myself but feared my addiction was winning.

Go to the meeting, go have some drinks, go to the meeting, go have some drinks, go to the meeting, go have some drinks . . . back and forth like that down Center Street.

As I neared Dry Haven, I noticed a long, imposing black Lincoln parked out front. A brilliant, shimmering black and white sticker on the shiny chrome bumper read "My granddaughter was killed by a drunk driver." The glare bouncing off from the sun light blinded

my open eyes.

My granddaughter was a year and half old at that time. She and her mother lived with us

briefly after her father was killed in a car accident. I had vowed to love and protect her. How

would it feel, I wondered, to hurt a little child? I climbed the stairs at Dry Haven not having

consciously made the decision to go in-- I was compelled to enter the building.

Feeling very shaken up, I hovered around the coffee machine for a moment in silence. I

wanted to be clean and sober or else I would die the same way I had lived-- lonely and scared.

But I also felt angry, like the choice to go get drunk today had been taken from me. I didn't want

to be an alcoholic. I didn't want to be the kind of person who would get wasted and drive a car,

despite the fact I had done so on thousands of occasions.

Two members I knew approached to welcome me to the meeting. I asked them, "Hey,

whose car is that out front? The Lincoln with that fucking bumper sticker. The one that says

"My granddaughter was killed by a drunk driver." Do you know?" I nodded my head towards

the front window.

They exchanged glances of curiosity and looked at me puzzled. I marched them over to

the window and pointed furiously outside. "That one!" I barked as I turned my head to look

where I had seen the parked car.

But there was no black Lincoln sitting there.

For the next hour I made rounds asking the thirty or so people in that room if they knew

who owned the vehicle with that bumper sticker. Not a soul in that room had seen that car on the

way in to the meeting that day or on any day before it.

I have looked for that long, imposing, black Lincoln and that brilliant, shimmering black and white sticker that glared off the shiny chrome bumper blinding me and making me see at

every meeting from Akron to Lima for ten years. I have never seen either again.

JERRY

On a Friday morning in July of 2000, a prior client of mine died at the age of 47 in a

nursing home in Findlay. After years of heavy alcohol abuse and deteriorating health, he had

been placed there by his family as they were no longer able to take care of him. Stooped over,

wrinkled, slightly discolored, and confabulating, Jerry had not looked or talked like Jerry in quite

some time. Though he could have easily been mistaken for a man approaching seventy, the

doctors did him no favor when they said Alzheimer's disease was responsible for his dementia.

Perhaps it will hurt less, they must have thought, than telling his family and friends he had

Wernicke's Encephalopathy or Korsakoff's syndrome, commonly called wet brain, or brain

sludge from years of drinking and drugging. Too bad. What purpose is served by allowing

fellow drinkers and druggers to believe there was anything natural, spontaneous, or unpredictable

about Jerry's death? There is nothing natural about having a brain spill out like Kool Aid into the

gloved hands of the coroner when instead it should jiggle like a jelly mold. This is what happens

to addicts and alcoholics who don't recover; they die. What could be more predictable?

Two winters before, Jerry sat in the brown reclining chair of my office one evening and

told a story which made me want to forget those things ever happened. He was two months

clean and sober when he told this story for the first time. I could imagine how his drinking

helped him forget until eventually his brain was so useless it just quit working and his body

followed.

Jerry entered the navy under the direction of his parents at the tender age of seventeen.

They thought it would "give me some structure," he said. "They thought I was out of control."

An intelligent and big man, standing six feet two inches tall, Jerry was a prime candidate for the

Navy Seals. Under the guidance of the Catholic school systems he had developed an instinct for responding to orders and was crazy enough to do, in the name of patriotic honor, whatever was commanded of him.

He was only eighteen years old when he landed in Vietnam and discovered his primary duty would be going in to the jungle and recovering downed pilots.

"This one time the Viet Cong had already captured a couple guys we went in for before we could get to them. We knew that eventually they'd take them to a camp where other prisoners were held. So we had to follow them. It took days."

"There were ten Seals in my party. We were tired and hungry. We stunk. But we kept walking. We staked out the camp, counted what appeared to be half a dozen prisoners and approximately fifty guards. We watched the prisoners, our soldiers, all afternoon before we could move in. Had to wait for night. You'd never forget seeing them torture those men. You'd never forget some of them screaming and begging. Some of them were too close to dead to make any noise. You never forget the sound of the speedy, sharp, foreign words to your ears. Their laugh. All of it mixed in with the sounds of the jungle, the loud silence in your head, the soldiers screaming only words you understand. Wondering if this is really happening. We came up with a plan."

At this point Jerry began crying softly, more like a whimper. The comfortable position he had taken leaning back in the chair was abandoned and he fell forwards slightly landing his face in his cupped hands. "It was so hard," was the last complete, audible, coherent sentence I understood while he told the worst of the story that night. He said it repeatedly. "It was so hard. It was so hard."

Whimpering made way to sobbing and talking made way to babble. From what I could gather, Jerry and the other nine Navy Seals waited for the Viet Cong to fall asleep that night and snuck into the camp. Without firing a shot or waking a guard, they were each responsible for

slitting the throats of five guards as they slept. Jerry had used the word "gourding." He

attempted to explain that he could only perform his duties by changing the language and "taking

orders." They successfully killed all fifty Viet Cong and rescued all six downed pilots.

"Going out, six guys stayed behind at various places along the way to booby trap

everything. We waited long enough for them and all sixteen of us made it to safety. We had to

kill fifty men to make that happen. Fifty fathers. Fifty husbands. Fifty sons. Fifty friends.

Fifty brothers," his lips quivered. "It fucked me up."

"I'm not a violent man, Bill," Jerry shook his head. "There are those who are able to kill

in the name of taking orders and protecting lives. There are also those who are forever haunted

by such actions. I've struggled considerably over the years with the memory of having to kill

those men the way we did. Every time it got too big, too hard . . . I just drank."

No one ever offered to help Jerry deal with what happened to him. He though alcohol

was his only escape.

I have so much sadness in my heart as I recall this 47 year old man who could have

passed for 70, in my office crying that night. This man whose life ended, for all practical

purposes, the year he was 18. The age at which perhaps some of us experienced as our biggest

personal crisis . . . what am I wearing and driving to prom? Someone died needlessly of

alcoholism on that Friday. Someone who shook my hands at meetings and tried hard to smile.

Someone who volunteered his first Saturday in July last year to help paint the walls at Dry

Haven. Someone who started getting lost on his short walks down there towards the end.

Someone who sat in my office one cold winter night and told me something he had never told

another human being.

Jerry's funeral was less than twenty-four hours after this death. The visitation was that very night. I would have liked to have attended both, but, like all his friends and acquaintances, was unaware either was taking place. His parents had tickets for a cruise which set sail on Sunday and didn't want to alter their plans.

Thank you for your lessons, Jerry. Rest in peace.

LETTER

Dear Bill,

Like a deer crossing a dark country road, paralyzed by the terrible screech of brakes and glaring headlights that blind her, I am frozen. Nothing in any direction looks like a reasonable option.

From my bath today, I looked up at the rack where your towel once hung. I thought of all the important things you said to me over the years. Why didn't I listen better? Why didn't I know then how much they mattered? Why didn't I realize, in the midst of my own storms, it would be your words that would keep me dry?

I may as well be a post-pubescent high school graduate all over again. I seem to know just as little.

My front left tire is low, as it so often is. You are not here to fill it. Some part of me wants to watch it deflate. Wants to drive around town in my Buick, tilting dangerously to the side, riding the rim, screaming "This is because my husband died!"

The streets are in the same places and they take me to the same places. But it all feels foreign somehow. You don't order a cheeseburger from across the table, "No onions, please." You don't push the cart down the aisle and turn beet red while I pinch your butt. You don't pull DVD's off the rack and ask "Did we see this movie already?"

The waitress has come to the table. "Can I get you something to drink?"
I want to order a Corona with lime. I want four or five of them.

I want to shrink into the red vinyl of this booth, will my muscles to deteriorate, feel my bones poke out from my flesh, and crumble into ashes so she can wipe them up with a lukewarm dirty rag from the table prior. I want to be forgotten.

"Diet Pepsi," I say. She doesn't know I want a Corona. She doesn't know you are dead.

I do.

I miss you.

Love, your adoring wife- Jenn

VASES

Believing them a colossal waste of energy, Bill made no room in his heart for resentments. For the duration of his 20 years of sobriety, my husband, hands neatly folded on top of his bed and knees firmly planted on the carpet aside it, prayed for anyone in need. He did not pray about them. He prayed for them. People he hurt, people who hurt him, people who hurt other people all got the same prayer: "My father, help them be happier people so they can be better people." He meant it, too.

Raised in a strict Catholic home, Bill struggled to come to terms with his own personal belief system versus the teachings of his religious education. Not infrequently, I could hear him mumbling in Latin from the other room, begging for forgiveness.

Several years ago, Bill came home late one night. He had been crying. "I went to talk to a priest," he explained. Having survived yet a 4th heart attack in the first five months of our marriage, he had never grown comfortable with his own mortality. My husband lived, a man grateful to see another sunrise, with the constant fear it may also be his last. Often, he was able to subdue that fear, give it a little place to reside in the depth of his mind. Perhaps in a crevice so private it required a combination. But I always knew it was there.

It was February 27, 2004 after a routine colonoscopy that yielded no concerns, when Bill started experiencing chest pains. He tried passing the afternoon watching TV, napping, and eating Nitro like Pez. No luck. A stubborn, and routinely avoidant man, my husband stood in the kitchen smoking cigarettes that Friday evening while I sat on his recliner, clutching my purse in my left hand and my keys in my right. "Can we go to the hospital yet?" I inquired every few minutes. At about 7:00 p.m. he finally relented, but only if I would drive him. He was not going in any ambulance. "Bill" I plead to no avail "I can drive OR do CPR, but not both at the same time."

The staff in the ER at Blanchard Valley Regional Medical Center saved his life. He had a heart attack just moments after arriving. Bill took on a smell in the days following that I would recognize again in November of 2009. He missed two weeks of work though the cardiologist was willing to give him four. But Bill wasn't helping anyone from the chair and he self-defined by whom he was helping. Long before, he came to terms with the reality that you can only drop a vase so many times before it is damaged beyond the point of repair. At some point, even super glue is useless. His own vase, the one he kept the dreams in for his former life, the one that held the dreams for how he would relate to his children, was such a vase.

However, it did not mean he could not yet help someone else superglue their own vase.

"Why did you see a priest?" I had inquired, not sure I wanted to hear the answer. "I needed to be forgiven" he said and went on for a half an hour or so. I did not really listen as closely as I should have. His explanation was vague, big. It scared me; I guess I had expected something specific, some crisis that could be named, defined. There probably was one, too. One that he had always known. One that could be held in his hands, firm and recognizable, like a baseball.

I did not respond to his need that day. I did not know how.

I did not make that mistake when the time came again.

FIRST DAY OF CATHOLIC SCHOOL

With my tiny hands in their big hands, my parents guided me into my first day of the

second grade at Catholic school. For whatever reason, I had not yet been baptized Catholic and

would not be until later, though my father was born and raised Catholic. My mother was

"reformed" in order to please his family; these are the scariest kind of Catholics. They've always

got something to prove and someone to prove it to.

Having come from public schools, I was not only nervous but completely unaware of the

new expectations. Fortunately, Sister Mary Batildha, my teacher, was a soft spoken and kind

hearted lady. She smiled broadly with her arm around my shoulder and introduced me to the rest

of the kids who were already seated. "Boys and Girls, this is William Hammer. Today is his

first day in our school."

The kids peeked curiously around each other to size me up. My mother gave me the "You better

be good Billy Arthur" look and walked out of the classroom door. My father nodded his head

and followed after her.

The rest of the morning was rather uneventful until lunch time and I let my guard down.

Unaware that a quarter bought a warm lunch, my own mother had packed me a brown

paper sacked lunch with an apple, a peanut butter sandwich, and some soda crackers. This put

me at a segregated table with a dozen or so other kids whose parents could not afford to buy

them a hot lunch. We sat there in that cafeteria, separated from the rest of our class mates among

our crinkled and smashed brown paper sacks, feeling different--wrong.

In an attempt to ease my sense of alienation, I struck up a conversation with a boy sitting

next to me. "Sure is quiet in here," I half turned my head toward him to observe his response.

Suddenly, my body was forcefully and abruptly pulled out of my seat. I had no clue what was happening and felt terrified.

The next thing I know, I am being chased out of the cafeteria and down the hallway by the large and punishing hand of Sister--I'm-not-positive who is whacking me repeatedly in the ass, or why. "You know the rules about talking in the lunch room!" her big and berating mouth shouts. "Now you have to go to the principal's office!" she smirks rather self-righteously.

A no talking rule--in a cafeteria of kids--eating lunch.

As I skipped as many steps as possible up the last set towards the principal's office, her door slightly ajar in ritual expectation, the sister gave me a particularly hard and painful whack on the behind. It released a belly full of unrest I had been trying desperately to control. I farted. Loudly. The sister made no mention of it.

I knew that I had to look forward to getting double at home whatever I got there.

This was my first day at Catholic school.

"I HAD AN ACCIDENT"

Sister Mary Helberg stood firm, focused, and squatted at the front of my third grade class

room, like she was cemented there. She was almost indistinguishable in her habit, blending into

the harsh black chalkboard behind her. Only the white of the trim across her forehead and her

pale, fleshy face separated her from the inanimate objects surrounding her body. A huge wooden

cross hung from her neck.

It was about 2:30 on Friday afternoon and my small bladder had reached full capacity.

For the last half an hour I had wiggled in my seat as quietly as possible, determined to go

unnoticed until the bell rang at 3:00. It was no longer working. Reluctantly, I raised my hand.

"Yes?" inquired Sister Mary Helberg as though I had interrupted the most important

lecture she had ever given.

"May I be excused to use the restroom?" I asked as politely as possible.

"It is too close to dismissal," she answered curtly.

"But I REALLY need to go," I pleaded.

"The answer is no, William." She enunciated "Dismissal is at THREE o'clock."

My bladder panicked. My legs swung. My mind raced. I was able to hold out until 2:55.

I lost control of my bladder five minutes before dismissal.

Fortunately, my seat assignment landed me in the very last desk of the middle row. By

the time my pants absorbed what they could, the bell rang. A puddle had just begun forming

under my seat. I putted around, carefully lifting the wooden top off my desk and arranging my

text books in an orderly fashion to buy myself some time. I left the room after all the other

students cleared out. No one had noticed.

It was a pleasant afternoon in late September; school had just started back up several weeks before. Were it not for the moderate temperature I may have escaped any embarrassment. I may have just walked home quickly and changed my clothes without ever having been worse for it. But the sunshine and relative warmth on this Friday afternoon brought what came next.

Here I was, scurrying through this tide of students, my body immersed and sinking, moving less like this wave and more like a breath held under the swell, only to be greeted on the front steps by my mother. I gasped.

She was accompanied by her sister, Jan, who was my favorite aunt. Her husband, Uncle Walt and their three children had come also. My cousins were all seated, smiling and glowing from the back seat of Uncle Walt's brand new bright and shiny white Ford Thunderbird Convertible. His hands gripped the steering wheel and strayed only to wave at me open palmed and inviting. They had driven with the top down from Detroit to show us their new car on this pleasant afternoon. And I had peed my pants.

My mother immediately observed the discoloration.

Her face changed and I heard the question before she asked it. "What did you do?" I remember thinking repeatedly, *this is all my fault.*

Knowing it would not satisfy her, I answered "I had an accident."

"What do you mean you had an accident?" Her thin lips curled.

I failed to respond. She demanded again, as though I would have a different explanation.

"I asked to go to the bathroom . . ." I stammered, "but she wouldn't . . ."

"Sister Mary Helberg would most certainly have let you use the restroom if you had asked. You're lying. You know how I hate liars." My mother did an excellent job of teaching me how to lie despite the constant reminder that she hated liars. She never let me tell the truth.

Without any attempt to comfort, my mother grabbed me and tied a jacket around my waist complaining loudly and flailing in exaggerated motions. We made our way to the car.

Aunt Jan would have done it differently.

My cousins all stared straight ahead, their smiles gone. They looked embarrassed for me. Embarrassed to have pee on my pants after school while my family waited outside in a new car. Embarrassed to have a mother like mine.

No one said another word.

MY FATHER

I grew up on the Cleveland Indians. My father listened to them play on the radio every

time he had the opportunity: working on the car in the garage, clinking around with the sink in

the kitchen, driving the car. He often avoided reality, particularly his marriage to my mother, by

disappearing into the basement or some other part of the house and tuning on the game.

Although born into a family of four children, my father was the only one to survive his

first year of life. Not surprisingly, he became a notorious hypochondriac. His constant

complaining about aches and pains was a vague and random, yet ever present component of my

childhood. He often wore the expression on his face of a man who is in some indefinable pain

and feeling quite sorry for himself as a result. It was his fear of illness and death that eventually

lead him to the doctor after passing quite a bit of blood the year I was thirteen. It scared the hell

out of him.

"You need to quit drinking, Joe," the doctor told him, "or else you're going to die." He

quit drinking all right. I never saw him pick up another drink again. But he was merely dry, not

what we would call a man who went into recovery. Instead, he got hooked on Valium, which he

took daily for almost twenty five years. I have a picture of my father when he was thirty four

years old. Though well over six feet tall he is gaunt and sickly, like he hardly weighs more than

one hundred forty pounds. He looks sad. He usually looked sad.

My father spent most of his life hiding. Besides the Indians, he also hid in a world of

gambling and alcohol. There were plenty of parties at home when Dad was still drinking. He

hung out with many police officers who came down to drink, gamble, and play pool on my

father's pool table. By placing a board and a cloth over it, our dining room table, which had long

since been replaced with a pool table could be converted back into a dining room table should my parents have dinner guests. The pool table served the kind of guests Dad had quite well.

I played the role of bartender, running back and forth from the kitchen with drinks for the guys. Eventually, I developed the habit of sneaking sips from their glasses and cans. Apparently this was quite entertaining for those at these gatherings. Now and again, they'd point and laugh as I got intoxicated and bumped into things. My mother was not humored by this. "Joe, you're a worthless son of a bitch!" she'd scream any time it was obvious I'd had more than a few sips. Dad then muttered "Jesus woman." He said little else to her--ever.

Perhaps it was this rapport my father had developed with the officers, or perhaps it was my interaction with them which saved me on several occasions in my adolescence.

One summer night when I was sixteen a group of us were out drinking and decided to scale the fence at the swimming pool. For whatever reason, we jumped in the water fully clothed. Eventually, some distraught neighbor grew tired of our drunken antics and called the police. Suddenly, the red flashing lights approached from the rear parking lot. Fortunately, our cars were parked in the front lot.

We all scaled back over the fence, hopped into the vehicles soaking wet, and took off down the street thinking our escape had been quite successful. Only several blocks later, however, we discovered a police car immediately behind us commanding us to pull over.

"Do you know how I was able to identify you?" asked the officer looking directly at me. We all shook our heads and gave blank stares.

"All I had to do," he said, pointing with his right index finger toward the trail of wet pavement behind the car, "was follow the path of water leaking out of the vehicle."

We were amazed.

Being a bit of a rebel himself and a man who would later become a friend to me and eventually die of his alcoholism, the officer gave us a stern warning and sent us gleefully on our

way. I remember thinking that my dad would be disappointed and embarrassed if his friend had

arrested me for drinking under age and unlawfully entering the city swimming pool. But more

importantly, this would give my mother another excuse to call my dad a worthless son of a bitch.

Though not an infrequent phrase in my home, I hated to think it was prompted by something I'd

done. He seemed so afraid of her. The whole business made my gut ache.

One of the few joys my father seemed to get out of his life as he aged was going to the

horse races. Every now and again my brother or I would agree to take Dad up to Toledo's

Raceway Park. One of us would drive him as he'd developed a series of more serious health

concerns including stomach problems and a weight issue. On one trip while in my early thirties,

I took a joint out of my front shirt pocket and lit it up in the car, right there in front of him. My

own addictions, which were not dissimilar to his, had kicked in and I wanted to get stoned.

"I know what that is," he said, and not a word more.

I didn't speak and proceeded to smoke the joint.

We were seated comfortably in the stands when Dad asked for an ice cream cone.

Though a rare indulgence, my brother and I both took turns making sure Dad got to eat an ice

cream cone on such occasions and Mom would not find out. He'd been banned from eating ice

cream.

Eagerly, I skipped down to get him an ice cream cone as this gave me the chance to have

a couple of shots before going back up. Already buzzing from the pot, a few drinks sounded

good. I took a beer back up, too.

I lifted my arm to hand him the cone, some ice cream melting over the side, when I saw

what looked like panic, even desperation on his face.

His voice grew hushed and imploring. "Please don't tell your mother." His eyes begged. I never told my mother. Why was he asking this time?

I wanted to cry. "No, pop, of course I won't say anything." I took several slow, deep breaths and turned away, my eyes not wanting to see more.

The horses started to move slower and the air got heavy and hot around me. *So this was it,* I thought. Already divorced once and unhappily married for the second time, this was what I had to look forward to in the years to come. The crackling sound of a baseball game on the radio in a dark and damp basement, cigars smoking and spilled beer on card tables where your friends play better poker than you and don't apologize too much for taking money you should have used to buy your kids Christmas presents, an unforgiving sun beating down on your balding head, and your pleading eyes piercing through the soul of your son while you lick an ice cream cone you had to sneak to avoid pissing off the woman you've said "I do" to for life. Holy shit.

That beer in my hand went down quickly. So did the next one and the ones after that. All the ones after that.

LETTER

Dear Bill,

Three weeks have passed since I was last able to hold your hand. I am sitting on the soft

scarlet sofa at Josh's store. It has been like a magic carpet, whisking me from our lonely home

and transforming me from a lost widow into a character in a fantasy film where Imps have stolen

time and with it, time's relevance.

Today I had lunch at Bob Evans and recalled the mornings we ate breakfast there so often

in the early years of our relationship. With Oregon berry syrup dripping off my spoon, I'd look

up at your handsome face. Your kind eyes wrinkled by the sadness you'd seen. Your graying

moustache and goatee framed perfectly around your boyish grin. The smell of your Caress,

Rightguard, and Lagerfeld intoxicating as it floated across the table and found its way into my

nostrils as if it were meant only for me.

Several of your shirts still hang in the closet. Before I crawl into the cradle of your bed

each night, I smell them. The collars that once visited your tanned neck. The pillowy white

cotton that slept on your strong chest. The sleeves that once hugged the tattoos on your biceps.

"Will you marry me?" you said simply, kneeling in front of me that warm May evening.

"Will you spend the rest of your life with me Jennifer Ann Cataline?" I recall how you fumbled

with two boxes as you could not decide on an engagement ring so gave me both when you

proposed. The stars peeked from behind sapphire clouds, eagerly awaiting my response,

witnessing the birth of our future. I said simply "Yes."

I miss you.

Love, your adoring wife- Jenn

25424696R00064

Made in the USA
Lexington, KY
24 August 2013